HACKING SCHOOL LEADERSHIP

WHAT MAKES TEACHERS HAPPY AND WHY IT MATTERS TO STUDENTS

11 ways great principals use happiness to create a thriving culture of learning in their space

HACK™ Learning SERIES

ERIKA
GARCIA-NILES

Hacking School Leadership
© 2023 by Times 10 Publications
Highland Heights, OH 44143 USA
Website: 10publications.com

All web links in this book are correct as of the publication date but may be inactive or otherwise modified since that time.

Cover and Interior Design by Steven Plummer
Editing by Regina Bell
Copyediting by Jennifer Jas

Paperback ISBN: 978-1-956512-44-1
eBook ISBN: 978-1-956512-46-5
Hardcover ISBN: 978-1-956512-45-8

Library of Congress Cataloging-in-Publication Data is available for this title.

First Printing: November 2023

CONTENTS

INTRODUCTION
Lead from Experience

I F YOU'VE TALKED with a teacher lately, you know they're tired. They aren't just tired; they are exhausted. As a school administrator and former teacher, I know that teachers are some of society's most hardworking and dedicated individuals, but lately they've been feeling the strain. The workload keeps piling up while resources dwindle, leaving them exhausted and overwhelmed.

In addition to collaborating, planning, teaching, assessing, and collecting data, teachers are expected to deal with non-teaching tasks, meet external responsibilities, and solve societal problems, leading to even more stress and burnout. And, as if things weren't tough enough already, the COVID-19 pandemic threw everything into chaos, making it even more difficult for teachers to do their jobs. It's no wonder many of them are considering leaving this career they once loved.

The pandemic highlighted just how crucial teachers are to our communities and how much they need our support. In addition to their already-full plates, teachers faced unprecedented challenges such as adapting to new technology, remote and hybrid learning, and social-emotional challenges. Yet, they worked to provide continuity to kids both educationally and emotionally. Sadly, their unwavering support of students has been met by continuous challenges and attacks on the profession. We owe it to educators to create systems of support, or we will continue to lose these amazing professionals.

One of the most significant factors in a teacher's decision to stay is to have a supportive administrator. Support, by simple definition, means working to minimize distractions by providing time, trust, and resources. And while administrators may have their own ideas of what that looks like, many of us haven't taught post-pandemic. It's time to listen to those doing the heavy lifting.

Teachers once craved a chance to be innovative and to be pushed and challenged by professional development and targeted feedback. Post-COVID-19, they just want someone to show up, listen, and appreciate them. Without teachers, a school cannot happen. Therefore, we must morph into the leaders teachers need now, even if it means changing the expectations of who we thought we'd be and what we thought we'd do as administrators. Some of us are flourishing. Some are floundering. It seems those struggling are holding on to old expectations in a new landscape. They are failing to listen.

And look, I'm not saying it's easy. As someone who spent her life in curriculum and instruction, I thought I would revolutionize education. And it's not that I don't still hope to do that. But I also recognize that I may need to press pause to rebuild a sense of trust and normalcy in the lives of teachers who were expected to hold it together during a time when it felt as though everything was falling apart.

As a principal, it's easy to get caught up in administrative tasks and forget about the experiences that led us to the role in the first place. Every administrator has likely spent time as a teacher. Some of us thought we'd never stop being a teacher. Reflecting on those invaluable experiences and using them to inform our leadership decisions are essential to our success in supporting teachers. Our time spent as teachers provided the perspective and empathy we needed to relate to staff and better understand their challenges. I'd even go so far as to say that this is the most valuable tool in our kit. By remembering and reviving those experiences, principals become more effective leaders and better able to support our staff and students.

Serving as a teacher for twenty years before becoming a principal is a career path I am proud of. This collection of experience allows me to think empathetically about each decision I make regarding helping teachers and centering students. This experience also means that I have been a teacher who has experienced working with a variety of building leaders. Some of my experiences with leaders helped teach me who I wanted to become. Others taught me who I didn't want to be.

I understand that my perception is based on my lived experiences. I did not teach in the classroom when COVID-19 hit. Instead, I took the leap into leadership. Throughout the pandemic, I tried to remain aware of what teachers needed by asking questions, listening, and learning. I turned my doctoral studies into an opportunity to look at what teachers perceived they wanted from a principal. My dissertation research, completed in March 2023, focused on whether and how COVID-19 changed what teachers want from a principal. What I do and what I write isn't just what Erika Garcia-Niles thinks. The contents of *Hacking School Leadership* come from research as much as from my experiences as a teacher and leader.

Like everyone, I'm not perfect, I'm messy, and I fail. Sometimes I fail hard. But I never stop trying and learning and listening and asking. It's difficult, and we often think we must do everything accurately, precisely, and perfectly. But leadership is messy and doesn't come with a roadmap or guidebook. There isn't only one way to do it successfully. As educators, we are often asked about our why, and for school leaders, it's so much more important to talk about the who. To be successful, we need to center on our people.

People-centered leadership is a way of leading with the teacher in mind. As a principal, it means centering your staff so they can center students. By building trust, empathy, empowerment, and a commitment to service, a principal addresses the increase in demands and dwindling resources in the teaching profession by focusing on the people and eliminating the distractions.

Currently, we have a lack of teachers entering the field and a growing exodus of those who have just had enough. This has placed education in a state of emergency. If we want to attract and retain teachers, we must hack school leadership to become the type of leader our staff needs today, not the type they needed yesterday. Hacking leadership is not foolproof. This book isn't plug and play. The most critical part of people-centered leadership is authenticity. It's not about a checklist or following rules; it's about loving your people enough to listen without judgment and to act consistently. The Hacks in this book are best deployed when combined with who you are and who the people are in front of you.

HACK 1

PRIORITIZE PEOPLE OVER PAPERWORK
Be Purposefully Present

*Anything is possible when you have the
right people there to support you.*
—Misty Copeland, American ballet dancer

THE PROBLEM: TEACHERS FEEL UNSEEN

I AM INCREDIBLY FORTUNATE to have a fantastic Personal Learning Network on X, formerly known as Twitter. I'm not sure how it happened. One day, I started tweeting about my love for what I do, and the next thing I knew, I had thousands of people rooting for me. I often leverage this community to tap into current trends in education, mainly to learn about generalizability. That's a fancy word I learned during my research, and it means that a topic applies to a wide demographic.

One day, I asked educators on X what they needed from a principal to feel seen and understood. People jumped on this question.

I received over six hundred responses. The bulk of them were from teachers saying that they simply wanted principals to get out of their offices and into the classrooms. Some teachers remarked that days would go by without seeing their principal unless they happened to go by the office.

The lack of principal presence creates a culture in which teachers feel unseen, unheard, and misunderstood. Principals are missing out on an opportunity to see how the little things that happen within the classroom walls are the big things that matter to a school community.

Teachers are, without a doubt, some of the hardest-working people in the world. Unfortunately, much of their hard work is summarized by the data accompanying arbitrary standards and mandates and the criticisms on social media based on limited or negative experiences.

What the world needs to see are the stories behind the numbers. What is happening in the classroom daily? What are the teacher's approaches to build culture and climate within a school? Unfortunately, we summarize this work by calling teachers magicians or superheroes without paying attention to the hours upon hours that go into creating these superhuman feats. In education, there are no magic wands. There are no capes. There are no invisible powers. There are, however, teachers who strive every day to be successful for the sake of their kids.

> *Principals are missing out on an opportunity to see how the little things that happen within the classroom walls are the big things that matter to a school community.*

Teachers have faced increasing criticism and scrutiny from a variety of sources over the past few years. This has significantly impacted their morale and effectiveness in the classroom. News, social media, and online forums have created platforms for school administrators, policymakers, and even parents to criticize the work of teachers publicly. The consequences of this criticism have been detrimental. When teachers do not feel valued, heard, and respected, their job satisfaction and motivation decline. They may become less engaged and experience more burnout in their day-to-day work. This, in turn, negatively impacts their students, who benefit most when teachers are engaged, passionate, and supported.

The negative perception of teaching and the frequent criticism have contributed to higher staff turnover rates in schools. Many talented educators have left the profession due to the lack of support and the negative environment surrounding teaching. Fewer people are choosing teaching as a profession. Consequently, the high turnover and low number of teaching candidates disrupt instruction, impact school culture, and create instability within the education system.

THE HACK: PRIORITIZE PEOPLE OVER PAPERWORK

No matter how wonderful some leaders might seem, we will never be able to improve the school environment or create a culture from behind a desk. Teachers want principals to understand the current realities of the challenges of teaching, particularly after experiencing the COVID-19 pandemic on the front lines of education. Teaching can feel isolating. Seeing the principal engaged in meeting student and staff needs creates a tangible connection that helps boost morale and build community.

When principals prioritize people, they ensure that they're meeting the needs and well-being of staff and students. This, in turn, leads to a more positive and productive environment. Teachers want principals who are in classrooms often enough to notice how classroom libraries are designed or what intervention they might use with a specific child. They want principals who know whose air conditioning isn't working, or who has a safety concern in the classroom, without being told. Ultimately, teachers want principals who see and understand what's going on in the school.

Yet schools are full of distractions. It's so easy as an administrator to get sucked into the work behind a closed door and forget about the rest of the world. It happens to all of us. However, if the pandemic taught us anything, it's that we are not guaranteed access to others. We should use this limited access as motivation to do the opposite. Instead of hunkering down in our offices, we could fling open the doors and step out into the hallways, parking lots, and playgrounds. Face-to-face interactions are like gold right now; we need them more than ever.

The pandemic and society in general have thrown a long list of changes at us. These changes have added challenges to the teacher-principal relationship. We need to prioritize the rebuilding of a supportive and collaborative culture if we want our building and—most importantly—our students to thrive.

Principals who prioritize teachers create teachers who can prioritize kids.

Not only is this good for the staff, students, and greater school community, as it establishes a connection and helps build psychological safety, but it is also vital for the principal. Most principals have been out of the classroom for some time. That's why we need to remember what it's like being in the classroom and why we fell in love with education. And we won't find this behind our desks or in our offices. We'll find it on the walkway in the morning, in the hallways during transitions, in classrooms during lessons, and at recess during play.

As leaders, we expect teachers to be present daily and to focus on building relationships with students, yet sometimes we fail to honor this ourselves. Principals can get to know students and start building trusting relationships by getting into classrooms, interacting with students, offering a helping hand, and being present during transitions. Students can only learn in places where they feel safe and know that they belong. The principal's prominent, consistent, and authentic presence helps develop this sense of safety and belonging in students, ultimately supporting teachers.

Each student needs trusted adults in the building. Being present is one way for the principal to get on that list.

While kids are our united reason for becoming educators, the prioritization of people can't stop with students. We need to make our staff feel seen and valued. They shouldn't have to visit the office to have a conversation or build a relationship with us. Instead, school leaders can be visible and present throughout the day. Seek ways to support teachers daily. You can do this in various ways, including conferring with kids during the lesson, offering a bathroom break for teachers, participating in a read-aloud, and ensuring safe transitions for students.

Principals who prioritize teachers create teachers who can prioritize kids. When human capital becomes the focus, teachers can focus on their students and provide the best educational experience. Schools are people organizations. The success of the school relies on the relationships between the people. Everything about a school improves when principals prioritize people over paperwork.

WHAT YOU CAN DO TOMORROW

School leadership is hard. Many tasks feel both important and urgent. It's easy to feel overwhelmed and try to take care of them in your office. Sometimes, it's just what we have to do. However, remember that nothing is important if everything is important. We must find ways to identify what we genuinely prioritize, and people are at the top of the list. People want a leader who values people. By being present, visible, and transparent, we build trust with our teachers in the most authentic ways possible. Here are a few ideas you can start right away to build trust with your teachers.

- **Hang out in the parking lot.** Being in the parking lot before and after school can significantly impact staff, students, and families. As a principal, you should be the first and last face they see each school day. When you spend a few minutes greeting people, you build a sense of belonging and connection among the classroom and the school.

- **Step out of the office.** Getting out of the office to engage with students, staff, and families yields more respect than when you sit behind a monitor all day. For principals who spend a great deal of time in their offices, this may initially be uncomfortable for your staff. Start by giving lots of positive feedback and praise to build trust. Even if you feel like you're neglecting email or being unresponsive, remember that personal encounters lead to better results than closing the door to your office.

- **Be transparent.** As a leader, if you have a week when you're less present than you planned, inform your teachers about the reason. Letting them know how you're spending your time is a simple and effective step that helps build trust.

- **Join the lunchroom crowd.** "Lunch duty" may sound like a chore, but it's an opportunity to build relationships with students and support your staff. Many conflicts arise during lunch and recess, and your presence can help relieve some of them. Building relationships with students outside of academics shows that you're interested in them as human beings. When conflicts arise, leveraging these relationships can help you respond appropriately and support your teachers. It also demonstrates that every job within the building is important.

A BLUEPRINT FOR FULL IMPLEMENTATION

Step 1: Identify how you are spending your time.

Many tasks fall under the job description of an administrator. Prioritizing people over paperwork requires proactive thinking about day-to-day activities. It might help to categorize responsibilities into significant groups, such as classroom walk-throughs, student connection time, professional learning, and professional duties. Brainstorm all the tasks you perform in a day and, if necessary, keep a record of them for a few days to compile a comprehensive list. This list will help identify your current time allocation and adjust it to prioritize human capital. Once you have an exhaustive list, sort the tasks into columns: With People and Without People. Image 1.1 shows an easy way to get started.

PRIORITY MATRIX

DATE:

URGENT, WITH PEOPLE	URGENT, WITHOUT PEOPLE

IMPORTANT, WITH PEOPLE	IMPORTANT, WITHOUT PEOPLE

NOTE:

Image 1.1

When planning your days, first place those With People tasks on the calendar. For instance, you can't do walk-throughs without the people. Therefore, prioritize time on your calendar for those to occur. Will there be times when they don't happen? Of course. However, we become what we prioritize. If we want to be present principals, we must make it a priority. If you don't block the time, it won't happen. Also remember that there's no point in beating yourself up if something gets in the way; tomorrow is a new day.

If a calendar feels overwhelming, use a daily to-do list. Prioritize the tasks based on whether you can do them with others present. This can help you stay focused and on track to ensure you address the With People tasks first.

Step 2: Stay informed and get involved.

Knowing about the day-to-day activities and events in the school is crucial for principals in today's challenging educational landscape. One effective way to do this is to stay up-to-date with teachers' communication and social channels, such as reading weekly newsletters, visiting websites, and scrolling social media feeds. By doing so, you gain valuable insights into the classrooms' daily operations and the challenges teachers face.

Building strong relationships between teachers and the principal is essential for creating a supportive learning environment and improving student outcomes. By staying informed about school activities, events, and initiatives, principals sincerely help teachers, build trust, and foster collaboration and teamwork. A culture of communication and transparency is also essential, and by staying in tune with the perspectives, concerns, and feedback of teachers, principals improve school operations and overall student achievement.

Specific ideas include:

- **Read weekly newsletters:** Principals can subscribe to the newsletters teachers send to parents. This way, principals can stay updated on upcoming events, school news, and other important information.

- **Visit teacher websites:** Many teachers have websites that contain interesting and valuable details about their classroom, including upcoming events, schedules, policies, and more.

- **Use social media:** If your teachers have professional social media accounts, such as Facebook, X, or TikTok, where they post updates, news, and events, then follow their accounts to stay informed about what's happening.

- **Attend classroom and school events:** Attend as many classroom and school events as possible, such as parent-teacher conferences, student performances, and sports events. This gives you a firsthand look at what's happening in the school and allows you to connect with teachers, students, and parents.

- **Meet with teachers regularly:** Schedule regular meetings with teachers to discuss their concerns, feedback, and ideas for improving the school. This helps you to understand the challenges and successes of the teachers and to provide them with the support they need.

Step 3: Learn beside them.

Participating in professional learning experiences alongside teachers models the importance of lifelong learning, showing a commitment to a learning culture. In addition, learning beside teachers keeps principals current and realistic. When principals know the targets teachers need to hit, they are better prepared to support them and provide relevant, meaningful feedback.

Professional learning is also an excellent way to collaborate with teachers and learn from one another. This leads to better partnerships and more effective instruction. Shared professional learning experiences build consistency with school goals and stronger relationships with the teachers we lead. (For ideas on how to personalize professional development, see *The Startup Teacher Playbook* by Michelle Blanchet and Darcy Bakkegard.)

Prioritizing professional learning opportunities with your teachers is a way to put your teachers first. The benefits are significant, and the shared experiences can boost student outcomes. Here are ways to promote collaboration:

- **Keep learning with teachers:** Create a schedule for attending workshops, conferences, and other learning opportunities with teachers to keep growing together.

- **Focus on what matters:** Ask teachers and check student data to determine what professional learning areas are essential for reaching school goals.

- **Collaborate and connect:** Plan group discussions or brainstorming sessions for teachers and principals to work together and build stronger relationships.

- **Learn from each other:** Schedule shared learning experiences like peer observations or book studies to work toward common school goals and learn from each other.

- **Keep the support going:** Give support to teachers after learning opportunities, like follow-up meetings or coaching, so they can put what they learned into practice and feel encouraged.

- **Keep growing:** Share your learning experiences with teachers and show that learning is essential for everyone to keep growing and improving.

Step 4: Host agendaless monthly meetings.

Being present on a scheduled day at a set time is easy and effective, and agendaless meetings are a great way to do this. You can alternate the times to accommodate those who get there early and those who stay late. You can also base the meetings around a theme. Serving coffee and snacks is a great way to motivate teachers to show up.

For these meetings, your job is simply to be present. Let your staff talk. Listen to them with the intention of hearing and understanding. Ask questions. These questions don't always have to be school-related.

One of the most effective ways to gain participants is to do this in an open-house format. Your staff come and go as they please. Hosting agendaless monthly meetings is a marvelous way to make yourself available in a manner isolated from teacher performance. It takes away the pressure of teaching and allows you to focus on the people instead.

Agendaless staff meetings break tradition; therefore, defining guidelines helps create transparency and consistency. Below are a few ideas to build these meetings successfully:

- **Set the tone:** Before hosting an agendaless staff meeting, inform participants that the meeting will not have an agenda. This allows staff to prepare thoughts, questions, or reflections.

- **Promote safe discussions:** Encourage all participants to contribute, listen without judgment, and respect each other's opinions. They are welcome to challenge ideas but not people.

- **Let the conversation flow:** Avoid predetermined topics and let natural conversations flow.

- **Foster a chill atmosphere:** Storytelling and laughter help ease tension and build stronger bonds among the staff.

- **Encourage honesty:** When your staff knows they are safe and encouraged to express opinions freely and openly, it leads to better discussions. Set the expectation of non-judgment.

- **Paraphrase the discussion:** Summarize the discussion, noting important points or action items to ensure clarification and understanding.

- **Follow up:** Communicate action items and take steps to implement suggestions.

Step 5: Take over the classroom.

While this requires planning, one of the most appreciated ways to be present for teachers is to get in the classroom and teach. Not only does this build credibility for you as an instructional leader, but it also gives teachers a much-needed break. One way to do this is to read a book to the students. There is absolutely no age limit when it comes to reading books to kids. Bringing your favorite book from childhood is an excellent way for you to help students get to know more about you. You can also carry on with the current class read-aloud, which is a way of learning more about what is taking place in the classroom. Showing up with your teacher's favorite snacks and sending them on their way will make them feel seen and appreciated. But, most importantly, giving the gift of time is a thoughtful way to be present. Image 1.2 shows a sign-up sheet that we use.

Grade-Level Teachers,

Please sign up for a 30-minute time when your principals can take over your classroom. During this time, you can enjoy the snacks in the lounge. We will do a lesson on Core Values for K-4. In fifth grade, we will work on promotion speeches.

- Core Value PowerPoint
- Core Value Google Form - alt link - tinyurl.com/valueGT
- Core Value K-2
- Fifth Grade Lesson Plan

Monday, 5/8

Time	Teacher	Teacher
8:45-9:15		
9:15-9:45		
9:45-10:15		
12:15-12:45		
12:45-1:15		
1:15-1:45		
1:45-2:15		
2:15-2:45		

Image 1.2: Classroom Break Sign-Up Sheet

Step 6: Be present for all stakeholders.

Being the principal your staff needs also means being the principal the community needs. The more trust you build with students, caregivers, and community members, the more you'll be able to support your staff. It's essential to take the time to build trust with all stakeholders. The deeper the community knows their principal, the more likely they are to understand that you support your teachers. This understanding makes complicated conversations easier when it comes to upset or angry caregivers. Caregivers often bring issues straight to the principal; however, if they know and trust the principal, they won't be surprised when you ask, "Have you spoken to the teacher?"

You can find many ways to build trust and relationships with caregivers and the community that are authentic to your leadership style. Setting up informal coffees for caregivers; visiting local churches, synagogues, and shops; and sending regular correspondence about the happenings within the school walls are ways for people to understand who the school leader is, what you believe, and how you are engaged outside the walls.

OVERCOMING PUSHBACK

Prioritizing people is undoubtedly one of the highest-leverage leadership moves; however, it can be difficult. Principals have a ton on their plates, and it may take a shift in perspective to realize that people are the plate. Without the plate, everything will fall apart (or at least slide to the floor). Teachers certainly want present principals, yet the reality of that can be tricky. It will take time for teachers to understand that the sole purpose of you being present is simply to be present. In the meantime, you may experience obstacles along the way, such as these three types of pushbacks.

So much paperwork takes time away from people. There IS so much paperwork in education. Just as demands and a lack of resources impact teachers, this imbalance also plagues building leaders. Doing away with paperwork is not an option, so you must find a way to keep up with managerial tasks while also spending time with people. One possible solution is to find a public place in the school where you can do your paperwork. It might be the library, a hallway, or a multipurpose room. Finding a high-traffic space allows you to continue working on your tasks while being present.

Teachers think I'm judging them. If you've been spending a lot of time in your office, teachers will certainly question you when you start showing up daily. You have to be transparent. Let them know that you are working on prioritizing being visible. Not only does this help them understand your purpose, but it also creates accountability for your presence.

As you work to build trust, keep your interactions positive. While you might not like everything you see, it's essential to be supportive and engage in ways that build bridges rather than destroy them. Depending on the size of your school, you will benefit by setting a goal. In small to midsize buildings, you can set a goal to visit every classroom, every day. For larger schools such as middle and high schools, set a schedule. A plan not only helps you to be equitable with your time, but it also creates the opportunity to build fair amounts of trust. If you're lucky enough to be on a team, you can coordinate your visits. Track where you have been and where you need to go. Do what works for you.

People will think I'm not doing my job. Unfortunately, principals aren't safe from impostor syndrome. More than likely, this narrative that people think we aren't doing our jobs is one that we are creating in our minds. I do it more than I care to admit. As long as you are staying consistent with prioritizing people over paperwork, there's no doubt that you are doing your job.

We live in a world of instant gratification and fast answers. So, you might fear that when people see you spending the day in the parking lot, the cafeteria, and the classroom, they will assume you have nothing better to do. Being transparent about how you are spending your time is essential, especially if you are switching priorities. This goes beyond simply sharing information. It involves creating an open and honest environment where stakeholders can trust and rely on the principal's actions and decisions. Having your words match your actions and building consistency around the belief that people are the most critical part of the school will help shift any negative mindsets.

THE HACK IN ACTION

I often say you never know when it's your face someone looks for in the audience. With that said, if you are a principal who spends the day in your office, there's a good chance your audience isn't used to looking for yours. It's important, for many reasons, to get into the classroom and out in the hallways. Not only does this action support the teacher and build rapport, but you will become that face someone looks for.

When I first became an administrator, I wanted to know so much so fast, and I quickly learned that I couldn't be everywhere simultaneously. While I did quick walk-throughs in each classroom daily, I also spent time in one classroom until I knew all the students' names. This was a helpful way for me to get to know the teacher and students and build trust with both. I loved hearing the students talk about me being in there. Others started to beg me to choose their class next. It finally reached a point where I had to pick a classroom name out of a cup so it was random and fair. This small act built excitement around my presence and eliminated the fear that some students (and teachers) feel in the presence of their principal.

I learned a valuable lesson the first year I participated in this one-classroom practice. I was sitting in the fifth-grade promotion at the end of the year. Each child read a favorite memory from their time at the school. A student who acted extremely shy and sometimes seemed uncomfortable in her skin walked up to the podium. She had been at the school since kindergarten, and her favorite memory was my time in her classroom. As she spoke, tears welled up in my eyes. She mentioned the reassurance of my smile and that she knew, no matter what, there was an adult whom she could trust if she had a problem. I had no idea that my presence had made such an impact. That moment changed who I was as a leader. You never know when it's your face a student is looking for in the crowd. This practice taught me that we must *always* show up for our kids.

Be proactive and intentional in prioritizing people over paper-work. This means cultivating solid relationships with students, teachers, and parents and actively seeking opportunities to connect with them. By doing so, you can better understand their needs and concerns and work together to create a supportive and inclusive learning environment that fosters student success.

Moreover, being present also means being responsive to the ever-evolving needs of our schools and communities. This requires a willingness to listen, learn, adapt, and commit to continuous improvement and growth. Whether it's through attending profes-sional development workshops, engaging with community stake-holders, or leveraging data and feedback to inform decision-making, there are countless ways to improve our schools and ensure that all students have the support and resources they need to thrive.

Ultimately, prioritizing people and staying present can create a school culture centered on student success, engagement, and well-being. Remember: we become what we prioritize. You can either be the leader who loves paperwork or one who loves people. It's safe to say the latter yields better results for kids, which is why we are here. While interruptions will always pop up, remember that interruptions are the work. Principals getting out of their offices and into the classrooms can be the rule and not the exception.

HACK 2

SEE THE GOOD
Gratitude Is Everything

Every day may not be good, but there's
something good in every day.
—ALICE MORSE EARLE, AMERICAN HISTORIAN AND AUTHOR

THE PROBLEM: TEACHERS FEEL UNDERAPPRECIATED

BEING A PRINCIPAL is complex, and the COVID-19 pandemic undoubtedly exacerbated the challenges. It's already distracting enough when we're caught up in the fires we constantly need to put out. What can happen as a result is that we fail to see the good. And there *is* good—plenty of it. Unfortunately, we often spend most of our time responding to problems, and this laser-like focus causes us to look for the challenges instead of the celebrations.

We see what we look for. Because we know it is our job to remove the barriers that hinder our teachers' ability to meet their students' needs, we become focused on what to fix instead of on whom to thank. It might not be intentional, but failing to acknowledge and celebrate the realities is a costly mistake for building leaders.

Teachers can feel underappreciated for a variety of reasons. With the quicksand of education policy shifts and curriculum changes, teachers may feel their leaders don't support them or value their work. Pair those feelings with the mounting workload, and they may feel overwhelmed and stressed, focusing on all that is going wrong rather than on all that is going right. And surely, a lot is going right.

On the flip side, toxic positivity is a phrase that has made its way into the world of education. It's the narrative that creates the "I'm fine, it's fine, everything's fine" dialogue we hear from some teachers. However, it's okay if everything *isn't* okay. We can't deny how hard this work is. Unfortunately, we fail to acknowledge the effort when we only spend time celebrating outcomes.

THE HACK: SEE THE GOOD

Teachers who are seen, recognized, and valued are more productive, engaged, and likely to enjoy coming to work. Wanting to feel appreciated is certainly not unique to teachers. However, teachers are often weighed down by the imbalance of demands and resources, making the simple act of receiving gratitude not just a want but a need.

Teachers give so much of themselves to meet the needs of others. Countless amazing moments take place every day in schools. As administrators, we need to retrain our brains to stop focusing on what we need to fix and tune in to what we need to celebrate. To do this, we need to consider who we are as leaders and who we are leading. Seeing the good must be authentic or others won't appreciate it. It needs to come from the heart.

Our brains are significant muscles. The narratives and stories we tell ourselves shape how our brains interpret information and how we respond to the information. We become reactive if our internal dialogue is about conflict and problems. If our internal dialogue is about gratitude, we become receptive. Gratitude has the distinct possibility of shifting and shaping the school culture.

> **Teachers are often weighed down by the imbalance of demands and resources, making the simple act of receiving gratitude not just a want but a need.**

Gratitude is meaningful only when given, so it's essential that we find ways to express our appreciation for the good. Communicate timely, precise, and sincere gratitude to staff regularly. This gratitude can focus beyond the outcome and also on the effort. Creating a formula for complimenting the good can be helpful. For example:

- What did you notice?
- What did it sound like?
- Who did it benefit?
- How?

This might sound like, "Hey, Brooke, I noticed when you were talking with Andrew about his choices that you validated his feelings by appreciating his passion for his toys. Because you validated him, you were able to build a bridge when it came time to have him rethink his behavior. I could tell Andrew owned that his choice was unexpected due to your validation. Thank you."

Having a formula isn't necessary, but it does help to ensure that the expression of gratitude is specific and sincere. More important than the procedure is the frequency of expressed appreciation. Good is happening everywhere; as administrators, it's our job to see it and validate it.

As a principal, it's imperative that we celebrate realities. This means acknowledging and embracing the current state of the school, including its strengths and challenges and the diverse experiences of the students, staff, and community. It involves recognizing and appreciating the school community's unique characteristics, accomplishments, and contributions. Celebrating realities is equally as important as celebrating success, yet we easily forget this in a profession bombarded with unfair metrics for success and attacks on the content we teach. Positive and inspiring moments are happening within the classroom walls, yet they can get overshadowed by negative press and narratives based on arbitrary standards. We don't want to be toxically positive, but we want to celebrate the realities authentically, precisely, and often.

Again, I know this is hard. But we all know it's important.

WHAT YOU CAN DO TOMORROW

Gratitude is easy to give and costs you nothing, and the benefit is remarkable. Our brains are wired to focus on what we want to see. To see the good, we need to recognize what the good is. That work starts internally. Take note of what you hope to see so you can identify it and replicate it when it happens. While a culture of gratitude takes time to build, you can start tomorrow:

- **Start a personal gratitude journal.** To train our brains to see the good, we can capture what we are personally grateful for. Our listed items don't have to be about school, but they certainly can be. While this practice doesn't instantly impact teachers, it does establish a habit of gratitude, which affects teachers in the long run. Administrators are constantly putting out fires. Therefore, much of the day revolves around decision-making and problem-solving. Creating conditions to reflect on the good helps us internalize our gratitude, which makes extending gratitude a much easier process. See Image 2.1 for a great visual reminder.

SEE THE GOOD

DATE:

THINGS I LOOK FORWARD TO	GOOD THINGS THAT HAPPENED TODAY

TODAY'S POSITIVE AFFIRMATION	WHAT I LOOK FORWARD TO TOMORROW

Image 2.1

- **Keep a notebook in your pocket.** It's hard to remember the good stuff that happens during the day when we're pulled in so many directions. A simple way to remember the good you see is to keep a notebook in your pocket. It may seem simple or silly, but it will undoubtedly remind you of the highlights of your day. If you don't frequently have pockets, the Notes app on your phone or even texting yourself can help you keep an account of the wins in your day.

- **Set a daily goal.** Setting a goal for yourself each day is a great way to hold yourself accountable. For example, if you start your day with three to five sticky notes on your desk with the promise to distribute them to the people and places where you see the good, it motivates you to look for the good. Make sure the sticky notes are gone before you leave for the day by either distributing them as you see something positive or waiting until the end of the day to complete them all at once. The second option has advantages because it allows you to end your day reflecting on the good that happened. Sometimes, as administrators, we need that.

- **Reach out to your community.** A quick way to learn about the good you can't see with your own eyes is to survey the staff. Ask them to share with you a positive experience they have had in the school. You can highlight these in your newsletters or share them in emails or meetings. Acknowledging and appreciating the great moments happening around you and then taking the time to share them is a relatively effortless way to express your gratitude.

A BLUEPRINT FOR FULL IMPLEMENTATION

Step 1: Learn staff appreciation styles.

Not everyone experiences appreciation in the same way. Some people love for others to show appreciation in public displays, while some find a handwritten note to be the greatest act of thanks (that's me). Principals can individualize their appreciation to the styles of those they serve. The more personalized the appreciation, the deeper teachers feel it and internalize it.

So, how do you figure this out? Well, ask. Finding out how people prefer to be appreciated doesn't have to be a formal affair. It can be as simple as asking staff to respond to the following prompt: "Tell me about a time when you felt appreciated." This gives you valuable insights into how staff members like to be appreciated and provides additional information about the individual's accomplishments. Principals can never know enough about their team. Knowing the staff personally and professionally, particularly regarding appreciation, creates an atmosphere of authenticity instead of compliance.

Step 2: Kick off the year with gratitude.

Can you imagine the difference in a new school year if you incorporate gratitude right away? While you may not know individual appreciation styles at the start of the year, you can still make your staff feel seen, heard, and validated. One of the best ways to do this is to make gratitude meaningful and memorable. You may want to start the school year with a theme, such as belonging. Then, for example, you can express gratitude by writing thank you notes highlighting how a specific teacher fosters a sense of belonging, the positive impact it has on students, and the atmosphere it creates.

Another creative way to kick off the year is through a personalized video. Ask students and families to share their wishes for a beautiful start to the year on the video and to thank the teachers for all they will do to make it a great year. They can send the video via email or through a shared platform like Google Drive. Showing it during your back-to-school staff meeting is the most personal way. Teachers love it when students are part of the new school year celebration, and students have a way of making everyone feel good.

Teacher Appreciation Week is an expected time to celebrate teachers, but it can't be the only time. They deserve more than a few days. Receiving gratitude can alter the recipients' brain chemistry. When teachers believe others appreciate them, their brains begin scanning the environment for signs of appreciation. It sets the tone for the entire school year.

Educator Charlene Gerbig leads professional development training on joy entitled *Reigniting Joy: Leading, Learning and Living with Renewed Purpose and Passion*. Participants take four to five minutes to write down everything that brings them joy and then identify items they do regularly and those they could do more often. Participants then set goals to engage in two joyful activities the following week. They are encouraged to pick an accountability partner who will check in on their joy journey. Starting the year off by celebrating the small victories and joyful moments and staying in the present with students ignites joy and supports social-emotional growth and well-being right from the start.

Step 3: Create a social media presence.

Social media can be controversial in the life of a leader. While it's true that it creates a myriad of challenges regarding students, it can also be one of the best resources for telling others about the great activities happening at school. Social media makes amplifying gratitude easy, convenient, and widespread.

Regardless of the platform you choose, you get to decide what you want the world to know about your school, who you are, and what you are doing. By seeking and sorting the good as a means to tell the school's story, your brain becomes wired to look for the good activities happening and to share that narrative. Here are a few suggestions for using social media to amplify gratitude:

- **Post public messages of appreciation:** Principals can use social media platforms like X, Facebook, or LinkedIn to publicly acknowledge their teachers' hard work and dedication. Post a message or a photo of the teacher with a caption expressing your gratitude and appreciation.

- **Share success stories:** Share teachers' success stories to showcase their accomplishments and inspire others. You can do this through short video interviews, blog posts, or even pictures with captions highlighting specific achievements.

- **Celebrate milestones:** Celebrate teacher milestones, such as birthdays, work anniversaries, or even personal achievements. A simple message of congratulations goes a long way in showing appreciation.

- **Use hashtags:** Create unique hashtags on social media to highlight your teachers' work.

Important: Ask teachers to share where they engage professionally on social media, and request permission before posting about them or tagging them. You want to respect their privacy, and they may prefer not to appear on social media, especially not on their personal accounts.

Celebrating the small victories and joyful moments and staying in the present with students ignites joy and supports social-emotional growth and well-being.

Step 4: Incorporate gratitude into everyday acts.

As a building leader, you get the opportunity to tell your school's story, which means weaving gratitude into everyday acts. You have many opportunities throughout the days, weeks, and months to incorporate appreciation into what you already do, including:

- Use morning announcements to highlight something or someone you are grateful for.

- Open your staff meetings with celebrations of the good happening in the school.

- Create a bulletin board in the staff lounge with positive shout-outs.

- End your meetings with positive closure by asking each staff member to name something they are grateful for. They can share verbally through a circle or confidentially on paper.

- Think strategically about how you can incorporate seeing the good in the building.

Step 5: Walk the building.

Walking around the building each day allows for countless opportunities to extend gratitude in person, and it doesn't have to be lengthy. A simple, "Hey, the gym floor looks amazing; I can tell you worked hard" can make the custodial staff feel appreciated. Look for the behaviors you want to be replicated as you do your walk-throughs; perhaps it's a student who picks up a piece of trash or a teacher who runs a lunch-bunch with students. The best practices to appreciate are the tasks that people do right, even when no one was looking (or so they thought, anyway). A personal thank you only takes a moment, but the impact can last a lifetime.

Step 6: Appreciate with your actions.

Appreciation isn't just about a positive sticky note. It's about the trust and relationships that exist beyond that sticky note. Teachers need to believe the words on that note to feel genuinely appreciated. That means you are present, know your teachers, care what they care about, and listen. If teachers are out sick, send a text to wish them well. If a teacher is hosting a fundraiser, go. If a teacher has a favorite activity or lesson that day, show up. But cut yourself some slack. You can't be everywhere all the time. Keep track of whose events you've attended, and make it a goal to reach each person.

OVERCOMING PUSHBACK

Some people may argue that there is not enough time to express gratitude in the busy schedules of teachers and students. Others may believe that teachers already receive enough appreciation and recognition, so there is no need for the extra effort. On the other hand, some may feel that forcing gratitude can make it seem insincere or even fake. Here are some pushbacks you might encounter and possible responses.

There's never enough time. It's not that we don't appreciate the beautiful acts around us. It's just that sometimes we get bogged down with managerial tasks that pull us away from seeing the good. This is why creating a gratitude habit is so critical. The small act of recognizing teachers is contagious for the environment and can potentially impact student learning. Making gratitude a habit or a ritual in your day helps ensure it happens. Start small and be realistic. Perhaps it's a quick note as you start each day or before you leave. If you try to go too big too fast, it becomes a hindrance instead of a habit.

My teachers already know I appreciate them. You'd be surprised. Many teachers feel unappreciated or underappreciated, and the negativity that seems to pour in from society isn't helping that perception. Even though a leader might say "thank you" regularly, appreciation isn't just about words; it's about actions. Appreciation can't be a one-and-done but rather it is an ongoing process that needs consistency to impact the school culture positively. Gratitude isn't just about a note on a teacher's desk; it's about building trust and respect so teachers know that note is sincere.

It will feel forced. The best way to build authenticity is to match up your actions with your words. Don't just appreciate someone for the sake of appreciation. You want your comments to be based on genuine feelings of pride. The more you work at building relationships with your staff, the better you are at finding qualities to praise. The more specific you make the praise, the more sincere it feels. Also, the more you individualize your appreciation to match the teacher's style, the more authentic and meaningful it is.

THE HACK IN ACTION

Recognizing and valuing individuals for who they are, not just for their job title or what they do, can significantly impact someone's life. And there are so many ways to say thank you, both traditionally and creatively. Over time, I've learned that gratitude is a powerful emotion that can profoundly impact everyone involved.

As a teacher, I appreciated the coffee mugs, markers, and notepads that accompanied Teacher Appreciation Week. While there are no bad gifts, some are better than others, particularly when expressing gratitude. At times, I felt that principals selected gifts because someone saw an idea on Pinterest or thought of a great pun.

During my years as a teacher, I wanted to feel seen, validated, and appreciated. I wanted to be acknowledged for who I was as an individual, not blanketed with generic praise or gratitude. So, as an administrator, I have thought about ways to make that happen.

One year, I asked each staff member to develop a word to live by for the year. I collected their words on a spreadsheet and kept notes of how that teacher exemplified their word throughout the year. At the end of the year, I hand-stamped bracelets for each of our staff members. Along with the bracelets, I wrote a note to each staff member about how they exemplified that word. We brought in a local coffee truck to serve our staff one morning, and I had a gift bag for each staff member with the bracelet and card inside. The number of tears was pretty touching. Teachers want administrators who see them for who they are, and I tried to do that.

A staff member who works in our after-school program didn't choose a word. She said that since she wasn't a teacher, she didn't deserve the appreciation. For her, I chose the word "family." I stamped the word and wrote her a note about how essential she is to our family. A few days passed, and she showed up at my door with tears in her eyes. She had lost her son earlier in the year. She expressed that there was a dual meaning of the word "family." Not only did I acknowledge the importance of her own family, but I also recognized her as part of ours.

The bond we created at that moment changed both of us and our relationship.

By recognizing and acknowledging the positive contributions of our staff, we foster a culture of appreciation, respect, and support that significantly impacts staff morale, job satisfaction, and retention. This, in turn, directly benefits students' learning and growth.

One way to do this is to create a system for regular feedback and recognition, where we identify and celebrate the accomplishments and successes of our staff members. This includes recognizing individual achievements—such as outstanding performance, innovation, or collaboration—as well as team successes and milestones.

If we want to retain and value our staff, we must recognize them for who they are and what they add to our school. We can't blanket praise across the school. We need to consider who the teacher or staff member is and how they like to receive recognition and credit, and we need to acknowledge the specific ways in which their words and actions positively impact the people around them. So much good is happening in our schools. We can retrain our brains to see the good.

When we prioritize recognition and appreciation, we create a more positive and engaged workplace that ultimately benefits our students and the wider school community.

HACK 3

PERSONALIZE PROFESSIONAL GROWTH

Make Learning Meaningful

What we learn with pleasure, we never forget.
—ALFRED MERCIER, FRENCH AMERICAN WRITER, POET, AND PHILOSOPHER

THE PROBLEM: THERE IS NO ONE SOLUTION WHEN IT COMES TO GROWTH

RECENTLY HEARD A teacher ask why professional development always feels like a punishment. At first, I was a little frustrated. However, the more I thought about it, the less frustrated I became. As a teacher, I had sat in so many teacher in-services, trying to focus on the speakers addressing topics that had nothing to do with me or my role.

And while I believe you get what you put into professional learning, I also know time is a limited resource. Teachers hope to foster curiosity in students. They hope to grow passion and build relevance to the learning. Far too often, administrators forget that teachers hold the same hopes for themselves, too.

Instead, we gather teachers together in a room and provide a generic set of information, hoping it resonates with at least some of them. And, yes, as an instructional coordinator and a principal, I am guilty of doing this to teachers, and I regret it while recognizing that sometimes it's unavoidable. However, when possible, we as administrators need to encourage curiosity, grow passion, and build relevance in the learning for our teachers.

District mandates, standardized testing, and national standards are factors most of us can't control. However, even when teachers and administrators find that they can't control the *what*, they often can control the *how*. While controversy exists regarding learning styles, we can agree that we have preferential ways of learning information—some of us love reading, some like documentaries, and some like reflection. We must get creative in honoring the adult learners in our building.

Generalized professional learning fails to consider teachers' individual needs, experiences, and learning styles. Just as we recognize that students have diverse learning preferences, we must realize that educators do too. Teachers come to professional development sessions with a wide range of prior knowledge, skills, and interests, and they require differentiated support to help them grow and improve. When this teaching is designed to meet the needs of the lowest common denominator, it fails to challenge or engage more experienced teachers or, conversely, may overwhelm those who are struggling. As a result, one-size-fits-all professional learning feels irrelevant, disengaging, and ineffective.

THE HACK: PERSONALIZE PROFESSIONAL GROWTH

As adults, if we want to learn something, we Google it, YouTube it, or TikTok it. I have taught myself how to make cookie dough balls out of chickpeas that actually taste good, thanks to TikTok. Now, if that isn't magic ...

With a world full of information at our fingertips, it's essential for us to think about professional learning in a way that honors where teachers are today, which is much different than where they were five years ago. Access to learning has changed. We need to be willing to change, too.

We need to prioritize differentiated, personalized professional learning that respects and responds to the unique needs and goals of each teacher.

While most principals would agree that high levels of student learning are essential, we almost never agree on how to get there. This is partly because teachers are all over the spectrum in where they are in their own learning. Teachers come to us with various experiences and skills. In addition, they are different humans with varied innate skill sets. We owe it to teachers to create experiences that work with their unique learning styles, interests, desires, hopes, and passions. The only way to do this is to stop focusing on compliant, boxed professional learning and to offer teachers a voice and choice. Then, we need to give them time to do the learning.

That bears repeating ... then, we need to give them *time* to do the learning.

Mandates and initiatives make it difficult to choose what teachers are learning. Still, we typically have some flexibility in how teachers learn. If teachers do the same thing in lockstep, they miss out on the opportunities for authentic collaboration, ideas, and—most importantly—passion. As building leaders, this means letting go of the type of instructional leader we thought we would be and focusing on becoming a facilitator of learning experiences. This is hard for some but necessary if you want to honor your teachers as individuals.

> *We need to prioritize differentiated, personalized professional learning that respects and responds to the unique needs and goals of each teacher.*

Personalized professional learning caters to the unique needs of each staff member, taking into account their specific roles within the school community while still appealing to all of them. Within a school's walls are classified staff, classroom teachers, specialists, coaches, interventionists, and more. There are few cookie-cutter development opportunities that truly fit everyone. Bridging the knowing-doing gap for educators is about providing context to research, apply, and reflect. Personalized professional learning focuses on the individual teachers and what they might need to deepen their knowledge and pedagogical practice while providing the context for precise application.

In addition to the authentic application, personalized professional learning also offers the opportunity for rich, relevant collaboration, which is the foundation of effective professional development. Educators bring ideas to the group that they are passionate about. Even when the content is different, the collaboration process enables teachers to brainstorm, problem-solve, and respond objectively, as the focus remains on the process and not necessarily on the product. Everyone still grows. But they grow differently. And isn't that what we want?

Personalized professional learning breathes new life into professional development. It is what teachers want and, more importantly, what they need to remain enthusiastic and engaged in lifelong learning and growth. While it might be outside the comfort zone of building leaders, this type of educational development meets the needs of each teacher without compromising the growth of all teachers.

WHAT YOU CAN DO TOMORROW

You can take minor yet high-leverage steps to start building trust, choice, and independence with professional development. Find small ways to build the autonomy you need to create strong personalized learning systems. Practicing collaboration and sharing individual learning experiences are steps you can start today and do tomorrow.

- **Flip your staff meetings.** I have a mug that says, "This Could Have Been an Email." More than once as a teacher, I felt like pulling it out in a meeting when I was overloaded with information without the time or opportunity to process it (I didn't, because I liked my job). Flipping your staff meetings is the simple act of giving information that staff should review independently beforehand, then using meeting times for processing, collaboration, and asking questions. When planning the collaborative activities to take place in the physical meeting, be sure to provide some voice and choice from teachers to ensure it is time well spent. You won't be able to flip your staff meetings tomorrow, but tomorrow you can start looking at your next staff meeting and divide the planning into two columns: Email and Collaboration.

- **Develop your personal learning network.** As a principal, it's essential that you stay relevant. This is the only way to ensure you are getting relevant and timely information into teachers' hands. Your personal learning network is key. Not only does this support your instructional leadership role, but it also allows you to be responsive to your teachers' needs. A personal learning network is a group of people you interact with regularly to collaborate, learn, grow, and share. I have found X to be a great source of information. I know others use Instagram and Facebook. Instead of just sending resources out into the universe through a mass email, share them with individuals you know will enjoy them, find them useful, and give constructive feedback. This means knowing who your teachers are, their interests, and what they might need.

- **Highlight the individual learning of your staff.** One way to excite your staff about creating their own learning experiences is to highlight the unique knowledge of your community. You can find a variety of ways to do this. One is via your weekly newsletter: add a special section to feature one or two staff members and the personal development they are pursuing. It could be a book, an article, a new skill, or an effective strategy. Not only does this allow people to highlight their passions, but it also allows your staff to see what others are learning. This will lead to collaboration, wonderings, and perhaps new passions.

A BLUEPRINT FOR FULL IMPLEMENTATION

Step 1: Collectively decide what is important.

It's essential to include your entire staff in the decisions about what is important. One necessary characteristic of a highly successful organization is to cultivate a common purpose. Instead of developing your school improvement plan in your office with the door closed (we've all done it; don't feel guilty), give your staff channels for providing input and feedback on the goals, purpose, and intended outcomes. For example, you may have three overarching categories: Teaching and Learning, Social-Emotional Learning, and Equity. Ask your staff to name something they hope to accomplish in each of these domains. You get bonus points if you do this through email instead of a meeting, and you provide safety if you create an opportunity to remain anonymous. Use this feedback to do thematic analysis about what is important to your staff.

Step 2: Create learning collections.

Collecting resources that address your school's goals is a great way to kickstart and maintain learning. Think about books (perhaps including this one), webinars, podcasts, articles, and documentaries supporting the themes your staff is interested in learning about. Compiling resources is also a way for you, as the building leader, to vet the resources to ensure they align with your vision and mission. Vetted resources are a way to establish freedoms within limits.

You can create learning collections in multiple ways, and it's most important to choose a way that works best for your staff. While the pandemic was a friend to none, it forced people to improve their technology skills. Here are a few ways to create learning connections:

- **Digital Folders:** Cloud-based services such as *Google Drive* or *Dropbox* are great for gathering materials. Such services allow members to easily access and organize materials in a universal place.

- **Note-Taking App:** Apps such as *Evernote* or *OneNote* don't just offer a way to take notes. Learners can also use these apps to save articles and web pages.

- **Pinterest:** Collect and organize resources on a specific topic through a virtual bulletin board.

- **Learning Management Systems:** *Canvas, Blackboard,* and *Moodle* can create online courses and collections of learning resources. Schools can use them in many ways, including class-based learning or self-directed learning.

- **Binders:** An old-school physical binder or notebook is still a way to organize and store print materials such as articles and handouts.

- **Social Media Groups or Forums:** Groups and forums related to a specific subject can create conversations and put a wealth of information at your fingertips. Search your social media apps for relevant groups and conversations based on hashtags.

Step 3: Encourage teachers to develop a personalized professional learning goal.

Once you and your staff have identified themes, each of you can develop a personalized professional development goal that fits into one of the identified themes. The nonnegotiable aspect of each teacher's goal is that it must directly correlate to student learning. Consider the following criteria:

- What is the goal?

- What materials do you need to achieve it?

- What barriers do you foresee?

- What is the estimated time you need to complete your goal?

- What does success look like?

Image 3.1 shows a way you can encourage your staff to be specific about two personal professional goals for the year.

PROFESSIONAL DEVELOPMENT

NAME:

SCHOOL YEAR:

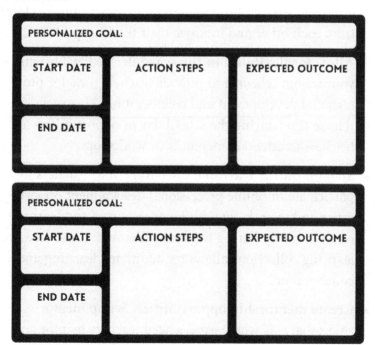

Image 3.1

Step 4: Prioritize your staff's professional learning.

Different schools and districts organize professional development in many different ways. Therefore, you need to consider how you might allow time for teachers to work on their goals. Here are a few ways to prioritize professional learning opportunities:

- **Provide regular professional development sessions:** Schedule regular professional development time for teachers to learn new strategies, best practices, and technologies. You can embed them into the school day. Teachers will *love* you if you can provide this learning outside of their planning time.

- **Encourage collaboration and shared planning time:** Create opportunities for teachers to collaborate and plan lessons together. This gives teachers valuable time to learn from each other and improve their teaching practices.

- **Allow for flexibility in the schedule:** Be flexible with your school schedule to provide teachers time for professional development and collaboration. This includes release time during the school day or opportunities for teachers to attend conferences or workshops.

- **Suggest online learning:** Encourage your teachers to participate in online professional development opportunities and to seek out additional resources and learning on their own. Sharing the newly discovered resources in learning collections allows for additional learning and collaboration.

- **Create mentorship opportunities:** Set up mentorship programs where experienced teachers mentor and guide new teachers, providing both groups with valuable learning opportunities.

- **Encourage teachers to set their own professional goals:** The freedom to choose what and when they learn—within the framework of your school's common mission—leads to high buy-in and a happier staff. Remember, though, that you must provide them with the guidelines, resources, and support to achieve these goals.

Note that these ideas won't be a fit for every school or every leader. Make sure that what you choose to do is sustainable for you and your team.

Step 5: Create collaborative experiences to share learning.

An essential part of personalized professional learning is to share the knowledge with others. You must create safe spaces for teachers to show what they know. Do this throughout the year in different ways, including these ideas:

Workshop-Style: Workshop-style professional development involves a pre-planned mini-lesson followed by time for teachers to actively participate, engage in collaborative activities, and apply new knowledge and skills to their practice, which promotes practical learning and skill development.

- Begin with a gratitude exercise.

- Share a relevant mini-lesson tied to your strategic school improvement plan.

- Break out for individualized professional learning.

- Come back together for a shared session.

Unconference: An unconference is participant-driven. The agenda and topics are determined on the day of the event, encouraging open discussions, spontaneous sessions, and peer-to-peer learning.

Before the Learning Day

- Plan how many sessions you will have and how many topics you want at each session. You can create a physical or virtual board.
- Prior to the day of learning, ask your staff what topics are rolling around in their heads and add their topics to the spots on the board.
- Plan which rooms to use for that day.

The Learning Day

- Welcome the staff and go over the day and the sessions.
- Hold attendee-led sessions based on your planning.

After the Learning Day

- Bring your staff together to share what they learned.

Learning Walks: During learning walks, teachers stroll around together, engaging in conversations, sharing ideas, and reflecting on a specific topic or instructional practice; this creates a collaborative and reflective environment that encourages professional dialogue, peer learning, and the exchange of insights and perspectives.

- Develop reflection questions about the learning and print them so you can pass them out.

- Partner up your staff members for learning walks.

- Give them time to go on a walk outside or around the building (depending on the weather) to answer the reflection questions you developed.

- After the learning walks, give time for feedback or reflection to understand what learning took place and whether it was valuable for the participants.

Learning Museum: A learning museum is a central space where teachers can showcase their learning through displays, providing an interactive environment for colleagues to explore, offer feedback, and engage in collaborative discussions. This activity takes place during the professional development learning time.

- Ask your staff to develop a way to demonstrate their learning. This can be a digital presentation, poster, display board, or video. The sky's the limit. This requires teachers to reflect on the content and ideas they absorbed during the learning process. Thus, teachers reinforce their understanding and consolidate their learning by organizing and presenting their knowledge.

- Set up these displays in a central location on the learning day. The act of creating displays gives teachers the flexibility to tailor their presentations to their individual teaching styles, interests, and classroom needs. They can emphasize aspects of the learning that resonate with them, adapt the content to their subject areas, and highlight specific strategies or resources they find particularly valuable. This personalization allows teachers to connect their learning directly to their own teaching practice, making it more relevant and applicable.

- Allow learners to walk around the room and leave feedback and questions about the learning. These interactions foster a culture of collaboration and mutual learning among teachers. Colleagues can engage in meaningful discussions, exchange ideas, and provide constructive feedback to one another. This feedback loop facilitates a supportive learning community where teachers refine their understanding, gain new insights, and generate innovative approaches to teaching.

Sharing the learning is not only an efficient way for you to review your teachers' development, but it's also a great way to spark interest and curiosity about additional learning from your staff. Just make sure that sharing doesn't add stress to your teachers. As you grow to better understand your teachers' unique qualities both as a collective and as individuals, it is essential to honor their preferences and consider their availability when deciding how they can participate in sharing activities. This way, you can strike a balance between encouraging their engagement and respecting their time constraints while also providing them with opportunities to offer feedback on their preferred methods of sharing.

OVERCOMING PUSHBACK

Many people are scared of change. They often continue to do what they know, even if it is less effective or outdated. Leaders can change the direction of professional learning, but they have to give up on the idea of expected outcomes. Remember that allowing voice and choice in professional learning is not easy, but it pays off in the long run. Still, here are three pushback comments you might hear or think yourself.

Accountability will vanish. Administrators fear they are unable to hold teachers accountable if they aren't all learning the same thing. To overcome this fear, you must trust both the process and the people. Many principals have spent their entire careers in buildings with traditional professional learning structures. They base outcomes on specific teacher moves instead of on teacher attitudes and feelings of satisfaction. This creates compliance over passion. Accountability is still a part of the professional learning process; however, what you hold teachers accountable for may vary. Instead of asking teachers what they learned, you might shift your focus to ask how they are learning or what they are excited about in their learning. It's refreshing to see how these simple shifts can change the energy of the conversation.

I'm not an expert in all the areas my teachers want to explore. Let go of the idea that principals must know all the answers to everything. You want and need teachers who know more than you. That's how we learn and grow. Our job as lead learners is to create safe conditions for teachers to become curious and confident about teaching and learning. Rather than know a lot about a little, principals need to know a little about a lot so they can be proactive in an ever-changing field. Get comfortable shifting your role from presenter to facilitator. And while this can be challenging, it's a necessity to develop passionate teachers.

Are we upholding district initiatives? It's no secret that schools face constraints based on district initiatives and mandates. Unfortunately, building leaders don't have control over removing these barriers altogether. Testing windows, assessment practices, and initiatives will always be there. As a leader, find a way to think creatively within the current context. Instead of going all-in all at once, find small shifts such as your building schedule or methods for teachers to display their learning. You will see that these changes significantly impact your teachers, their passions, and—ultimately—their students.

Instead of asking teachers what they learned, you might shift your focus to ask how they are learning or what they are excited about in their learning.

THE HACK IN ACTION

by Sarah Bombick, educator

This spring, we offered a Picnic PD to our teachers. We used the forty-five minutes normally spent at our faculty meeting to learn as a group. Because it was in May, we decided to make this an outside event. Each teacher received a picnic bag with a QR code and a link to their personalized professional development, snacks and sunglasses, and of course, sunscreen! We asked teachers to bring their technology devices, blankets, lawn chairs, and open minds.

Knowing that adult learners are much more engaged with their learning if they have a voice and choice in their work, we asked each teacher what they wanted to learn about (it had to be something that would impact student achievement) and how they wanted to learn it—via a podcast, an article, or a video. We spent the next two months finding high-quality, personalized professional development experiences for every teacher in the building. They could complete all learning using a cell phone or laptop, which continued to add to the personalization for teachers.

After participating in the Picnic PD, we asked teachers to reflect on their new learning and to provide feedback for future events. The teachers' appreciation for providing learning that was just for them overflowed. One teacher even mentioned that in twenty-eight years in the classroom as a teacher for hard-of-hearing students, this was the first PD she had experienced that aligned with her specific needs.

Even better, teachers became excited about their learning. They started to share their experiences with one another, sending out links to their PDs and posting them outside of their classrooms to show others. The energy and love for learning was contagious.

As exciting as it was to see how this motivated our teachers, it was even more exciting to see teachers using the practices they had learned that morning by that same afternoon. Teachers were engaging students in new ways with new ways of thinking. Because this event was in May, many teachers began to make plans for next year using their new learning.

Our teachers' engagement and passion for learning is a true testament to their love for educating our children. I truly believe this one small event has the potential to create a ripple effect that will impact so many students!

There is no one solution when it comes to personalized professional learning. Instead, giving teachers the freedom to choose their learning path makes them more invested in their growth and development. By offering ongoing learning opportunities, you help teachers enhance their instructional practices and adapt to the evolving needs of their students, ultimately leading to improved student outcomes. In addition, personalized professional learning can help teachers stay current with the latest research, teaching strategies, and technologies. This also promotes flexible thinking and fosters a culture of continuous improvement.

Personalized professional learning doesn't have to be expensive or time-consuming. Many free and low-cost resources such as webinars, podcasts, and online courses are available. Schools can also leverage the expertise of their staff by creating a culture of sharing and collaboration. This saves time and money and, more importantly, builds a stronger sense of community while also honoring each teacher's unique needs and interests.

It's also valuable to recognize that sometimes staff need consistent messaging. Finding even small ways to incorporate choice into their learning makes a big impact, even if it feels small.

HACK 4

BALANCE INITIATIVES
Decide What's Important;
Let Go of What's Not

*Too many professional development initiatives are
done to teachers—not for, with, or by them.*
—ANDY HARGREAVES, RESEARCHER, WRITER, SPEAKER, AND CHANGE AGENT

THE PROBLEM: TOO MANY INITIATIVES
LEAD TO OVERLOAD

TEACHERS ARE LEAVING the profession in droves ... many for the same reason: an imbalance between demands and resources. Basically, so much is expected of them, and they aren't always supported. If you want the specifics, get on any social media site, search for this topic, and read the comments. It's so heartbreaking that I don't read them anymore. New initiatives are piled on top of old initiatives with nothing taken away, leaving a lack of clarity on what teachers should be doing and whether it's working.

Initiative overload is how many educators describe the current state of education. While it likely comes from a goal of wanting the best for our kids, we sometimes forget that effective change takes time, planning, and—most importantly—people. Something has to give. As team management author Patrick Lencioni says, "If everything is important, then nothing is."

Often, initiatives focus on improving processes instead of people. This is a fatal flaw in the cycle of change. We implement programs instead of considering who our people are and how to build their skill sets. Too much is going on in education. If we want to support teachers, we must find ways to *remove* initiatives. Sometimes our pride gets in the way of doing so because we spent resources and have nothing to show for it. As leaders, we must be willing to let go of mistakes, even if it has taken us a while to make them.

With initiatives, we can have too much of a good thing. What begins with the best of intentions can lead to overload, confusion, and a divided school focus. Time, energy, and resources end up going in different directions and toward different goals and areas of improvement.

And—yet another weakness—in some instances, we have built person-dependent initiatives that failed because we didn't develop systems for maintaining them. As a result, people couldn't carry out the initiatives since they either didn't understand them or didn't believe in them.

> **If we want to support teachers, we must find ways to remove initiatives.**

All this leads to a lack of progress and success, further discouraging teachers. Teachers and schools become confused about what to prioritize, and they focus on the wrong goals, leading to burnout and decreased motivation. This often leaves teachers without the time, energy, or desire to work on the right thing.

Simply put, when teachers are frustrated, they don't have buy-in.

THE HACK: BALANCE INITIATIVES

Ending initiative overload is crucial to teachers and their well-being. And, yes, this may mean letting go of the ideas we want to focus on so we can focus on the ideas we need to focus on. That's hard. I recognize that. However, I also recognize that we need teachers. If we want to keep teachers in the profession, we need to balance our initiatives.

The fastest way to end initiative overload is to say no to new initiatives. Unfortunately, fastest doesn't always mean best. Leaders can prioritize working collaboratively with their staff to balance what new initiatives they can take on and what old ones they can eliminate by establishing a system for evaluating the importance of each initiative.

First, define the nonnegotiables. One way to do this is to have a filter when considering initiatives. Two simple questions can help determine if it's worth examining:

- Could this be beneficial to our kids?

- Will this positively impact our school?

If the answer to either of those questions is no, perhaps the answer should be no. If an initiative does not benefit students or the school community as a whole, it should be put on hold, even if it's really, really fun and exciting.

Identify the most critical areas of focus and prioritize and align initiatives around those areas to make progress and achieve success. Then create a clear plan and timeline for all initiatives to ensure you implement them effectively and sustainably. Additionally, principals should consider whether the initiative is feasible, considering available resources, staff capacity, and reasonable timelines. The key word here is reasonable. Image 4.1 is an easy visual for putting this in perspective.

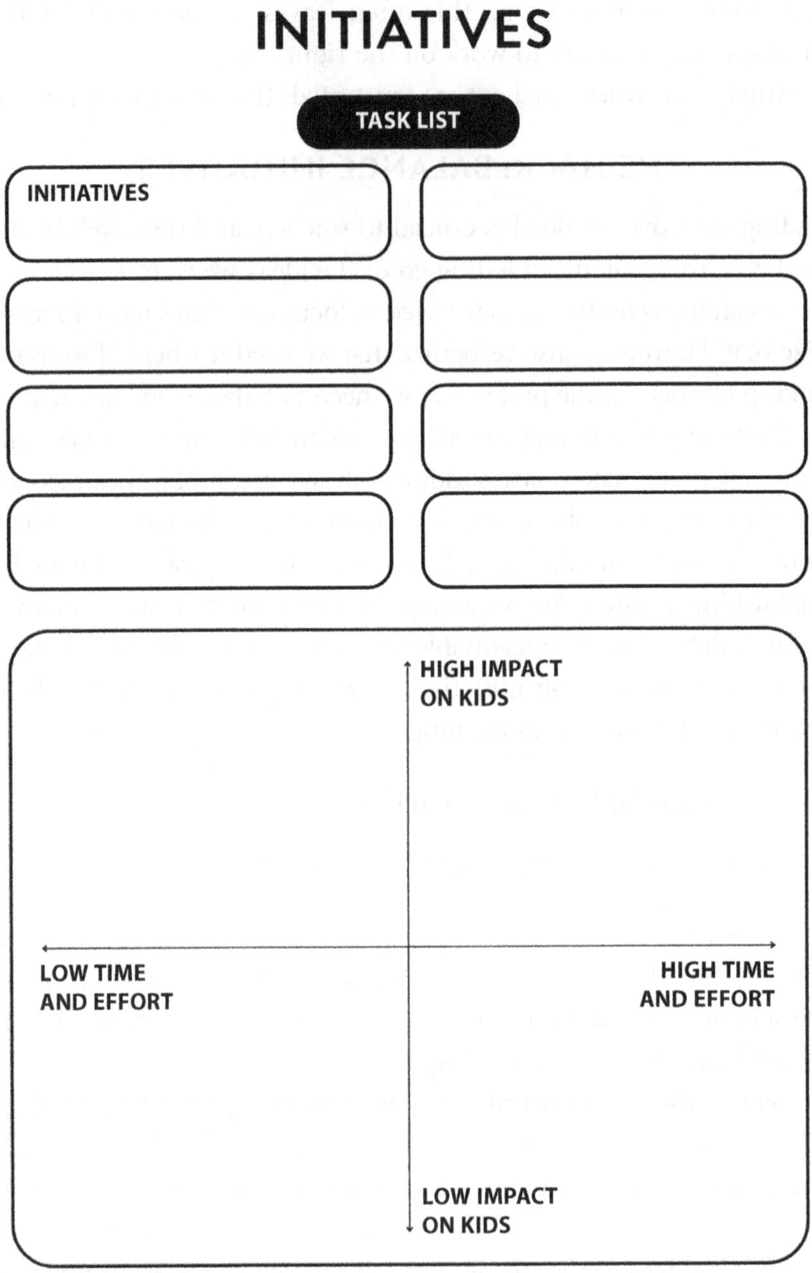

INITIATIVES

TASK LIST

INITIATIVES

HIGH IMPACT
ON KIDS

LOW TIME
AND EFFORT

HIGH TIME
AND EFFORT

LOW IMPACT
ON KIDS

Image 4.1: Evaluating Initiatives

Involving stakeholders in the process of balancing initiatives is a must. Believe it or not, we are full of bias. We need that system of checks and balances that teachers, staff, community, and students provide. In order for stakeholders to provide input into initiatives, they must know and understand the shared vision for the school. This way, they help ensure that initiatives align with the school's goals and mission and address areas of need.

Strategies for prioritizing lead to greater buy-in, and with greater buy-in comes success. These decisions are clearer when we keep our kids at the center of all initiatives.

Remember: initiatives don't have to be brand-new. Some of the best ones are built on existing successes. The key is to prioritize initiatives that don't throw away the work that your educators have already done ... as long as it's still the right work. With that, it's essential to have a good system for evaluating initiatives' relevance and success. Assessing and measuring help you adjust when needed and reallocate necessary resources to ensure you collectively meet your updated goals.

As leaders, we can strike a balance. When we are mandating or implementing a new initiative, we need to find an activity we can remove from teachers' plates. In other words, we need to shift the imbalance between demand and resources. With each new ask, we need to figure out where we will get the time to develop this new initiative. It can't be with new time; it has to fit within our current structure. And we need the time to do it well.

WHAT YOU CAN DO TOMORROW

While eliminating initiatives takes time, you can do a few activities right away to begin thinking about what your priorities are and, even more importantly, what they are not. Prioritize initiatives that fit with where you are now and where you want to go, and let go of the initiatives that no longer match your vision and mission. This can be a challenge, as often, these initiatives either once seemed important or you spent a long time on them. However, you can't keep everything. Decide where you are by following these suggestions.

- **Make a list of all the initiatives happening now in your building.** To prioritize them, you must have a clear view of what they are. Start by listing the initiatives currently required of your teachers. It helps to sort them into categories such as procedural and instructional. Once you have a list, highlight those that fall within your current school improvement plan. This gives you an idea of what you need to prioritize.

- **Survey your teachers.** Sometimes what you think is essential isn't necessary to teachers. This means you haven't adequately communicated your vision and mission, or you've outgrown your past ideas or thinking. A quick way to do a temperature take on where your teachers are with initiatives is to ask them to list the top three priorities of the building. You can use a simple survey such as a Google Form to collect this data. Once you have the results, do a thematic analysis to find the gaps between what you and your staff think is important.

- **Say no.** The best way to avoid initiative overload is to stop it before it happens. Many principals are people-pleasers. It can be challenging to say no. However, the more you say yes, the greater the risk that you will burn your teachers out. It's important to say no to the things that don't fit within your school's vision and mission or are not your top priorities at this time.

  It's vital not only for you as the building leader to say no but also to model saying no. Much like administrators, teachers are people-pleasers. They take on too much to avoid disappointing someone or being seen in a negative light (I'm so guilty). Show teachers that saying no is acceptable. It might even be helpful to weave saying no into your professional development. It seems silly, but many teachers struggle with this skill. Building a culture where "no" is okay can only happen if you are willing to say it yourself.

A BLUEPRINT FOR FULL IMPLEMENTATION

Step 1: Define your nonnegotiables.

State and district mandates are not going away, and we don't have the option to get rid of them. That makes them nonnegotiable. In addition, we may want to incorporate other initiatives, but they may not be feasible right now. As leaders, we need to define our nonnegotiables. You will lose a lot of trust if you bring something to the table, ask for feedback, and then later on decide that you will require teachers to carry it through as prescribed. It's imperative that you categorize the musts, the shoulds, and the what-might-be-fun-to-dos.

Step 2: Filter your initiatives.

When deciding on programs or actions you want your staff to implement, it's essential to filter what you let through. This shouldn't be you alone in a room making decisions; include your staff in defining what the filter is and what passes through. For example, a filter might be, "Does this positively impact each student and all students?" If the answer is no, it might not be the right choice or time to implement. Think about this in terms of an hourglass. At the top is everything we want or have to do. The middle is our filter. The bottom of the hourglass is filled with the initiatives that pass the filter. This provides a visual, direction, and priorities for your upcoming year.

Also consider the feasibility and resources needed to implement each initiative. Ask yourself questions such as, "Is this feasible given our budget and staffing constraints?" and "Do we have the necessary resources to make this happen?" The validated practicality of each initiative ensures that your staff can successfully implement it.

Another factor to consider is alignment with your organization's core beliefs. Ask yourself, "Does this initiative align with our mission and values?" If it doesn't, it may not fit.

Finally, be flexible with your filter. As circumstances change, you may need to adjust the filter to ensure your initiatives remain relevant and impactful. Regularly review and update your filter to check that your initiatives are aligned with your organization's goals, values, and priorities.

Step 3: Create all internal systems.

The more systemic we are with initiatives, the easier it is to identify what is essential, what is going well, and what might need to change. When we introduce a new initiative, the plan should identify and include who will be involved and how, what the expenses are in terms of resources, what barriers might be in the way, and the specific action steps. Defining these specifics is vital to teachers because they want to know how this will impact their day-to-day operations. Having a system allows teachers to wrap their brains around the practical applications. Too often, when introducing new initiatives, administrators announce them to teachers while we are still in the process of thinking about the *how*.

Building an internal system means having the following:

- **Aligned goals and outcomes:** Define how the new initiative fits into what you are currently doing and who you hope to become. This definition should include the rationale or the why.

- **A plan for communication:** Communicate early and often. Transparency is vital to teachers even when you don't have all the answers.

- **A specific plan for implementation:** This plan should include the what, when, and how. Outlining specifics enables teachers to plan how it fits into what they are doing now and in the future.

Step 4: State beginning, review, and end dates for initiatives.

Sometimes we throw new initiatives out to our staff but don't define a clear timeline, a metric for success, or a process for review or feedback (I'm so guilty). Metrics are vital to decide whether the initiative still fits your current vision and mission. In this, remind yourself that it's okay to let go of the mistakes. For example, if a reading intervention you implemented isn't driving growth for your students, you need to let it go, even if the school has been doing it for years.

Building beginning, review, and end dates into initiatives is a systematic way to ensure they are implemented with fidelity and that you can make changes if they aren't meeting the intended outcome.

Step 5: When you add something new, define what you let go.

One of the most emphatic requests teachers make is that if administrators give them something new to do, they need to find something to remove. Teachers are right about this. When we try to do everything, we do nothing well. When you are planning to implement new initiatives, part of the process should be to respond collectively to the following prompt: "If we want to _____, then we need to stop _____, because _____.

Note: The reason we end an initiative can't just be because it's complex or time-consuming. We need to make evidence-based, child-centered, and data-driven decisions.

> **When we try to do everything, we do nothing well.**

OVERCOMING PUSHBACK

If school leaders feel passionate about one thing, it's their initiatives. It's good to feel passionate about what we plan to try and do; however, this passion can't overshadow current realities. More than anything, if we want teachers to support new, valuable initiatives, we need to build a collective understanding and belief. Here are a few common pushbacks you may face.

We need change now. Systemic change certainly takes time. And we are all short on time. Remember that change is not an event; it's a process. When leaders try to implement change, they often share the *what* without the *why* or the *how* because they want it to happen immediately. When they do this, initiatives become about compliance, turning them into *one more thing* instead of *the most important thing.* Getting feedback from teachers, taking time to lay out a solid plan, and figuring out what to let go of are definitely harder on the front end. Still, they save time and energy on the back end as the teachers will understand what they are doing, their part, and why you're doing it.

Everything is important. Even if everything is important, not everything is urgent. In addition, not everything is important to everyone. Using a clear system to prioritize initiatives helps determine which ideas have a broad impact, are easy to implement, and are urgent. Sometimes we are so excited or anxious to start new projects or ideas that we forget to ensure they are the right ones. We must sift them through our filter to know how they fit with where we are and where we hope to go as an organization. We also need to ensure they have a broad, not isolated, impact. This is much easier when we create a universal process for determining which initiatives to prioritize and implement.

They won't listen. Sometimes leaders get frustrated because they have told their staff why they are doing something, but the teachers can't articulate it when asked. Their lack of ability to articulate isn't because of *what* we are telling them but rather *how* we are telling them. When we don't work to build collective understanding regarding the need for an initiative, the justification lives with us instead of with our teachers. Teachers need to be part of the implementation of initiatives, so facilitate the building schema and background information. In addition, listen to the pushback. Leaders are often the facilitators of the changes rather than the people living with the changes. You need your teachers' voices in the space.

THE HACK IN ACTION

When I first came to my building as principal, the staff was divided over our equity work. Knowing that this work is essential, I looked for a way to unite us. That meant prioritizing initiatives that would help us invest in the work in a way that would move everyone forward.

First, I assessed the school's needs by talking to teachers, staff, parents, and students. I discovered that we were having such a hard time with equity work because we were focusing on what we were against rather than what we were for. People were told that only certain beliefs and thinking were right, taking away from the authenticity of who they were.

Second, defining who we wanted to be as a school culture was critical to gaining staff buy-in, so we used our staff meetings to create a collective mission. Rather than center on what we were against, we centered on what we wanted to become. Our mission: to become a place where everyone feels belonging without compromising.

Third, we wanted to ensure our students had a shared understanding of our mission. With input from students, staff, and families, we developed lessons to be taught throughout the school so students would have shared learning and experiences around the idea of belonging. Involving community members in deciding what to prioritize made a big difference in support and buy-in.

Fourth, we created a way to measure belonging for our staff and students through a four-question survey:

1. Do you feel like this is the school for you?

2. Do you feel like you can be your true self here?

3. Do you have a trusted person you can talk to when there is a problem?

4. Are you treated the way you want to be treated?

As our work moved forward, teachers began to feel at ease with our efforts. Our survey data started to improve. Most importantly, our staff and students became comfortable expressing who they were.

Our culture and climate improved by collectively defining what we wanted to prioritize. The staff supported this work simply because we defined what we were working for rather than against. Since then, building belonging has become the underlying thread that connects our initiatives.

Balancing initiatives involves effectively managing and prioritizing various programs, ideas, and goals within a school. Ensuring the initiatives align with the school's mission and values, allocating resources accordingly, and evaluating the success and impact of these initiatives are essential steps to balancing those we implement.

It can't, nor should it, be the sole responsibility of the principal to make decisions about initiatives. Involving stakeholders such as teachers, staff, and families in the decision-making process is vital to its success and ensures balance. We may not be able to carry out every initiative we feel passionate about, but we can execute the most important ones well. It's all about balance.

HACK 5

FOCUS ON WELL-BEING

Recognize Teachers' Social-Emotional Needs

I have come to believe that caring for myself is not self-indulgent. Caring for myself is an act of survival.
—AUDRE LORDE, WRITER, FEMINIST, AND CIVIL RIGHTS ACTIVIST

THE PROBLEM: OUR TEACHERS ARE STRESSED OUT

STRESS IN THE field of education is not a new phenomenon. Teachers experienced it long before the COVID-19 pandemic, but it certainly exacerbated the challenges and pressures. Throughout the past few years, educators have experienced additional stress, trauma, and burnout from the impacts of balancing the ever-changing demands of their personal and professional lives.

According to a study by the American Federation of Teachers, 78 percent of teachers reported feeling physically and emotionally drained at the end of the day, and 61 percent said their work was always or often stressful.

These pressures are not only detrimental to the health and well-being of teachers but can also hurt student outcomes. When teachers are overworked and overloaded, they may be unable to provide the support and attention their students need. Additionally, teachers who are experiencing burnout may be more likely to leave the profession, which can lead to teacher shortages that further exacerbate the problem.

Often, teachers carry the social-emotional load, not only for their own families but also for their students. They are working hard to be strong for those within their care, which comes at the expense of their mental well-being. While this certainly doesn't go unnoticed, many teachers have found that the efforts of administrators are inconsistent—words don't match actions. As leaders, we say things such as, "Take care of yourself" or "You can't pour from an empty pitcher." Yet then we ask them to attend meetings, learn new instructional practices, answer countless emails, and sub for colleagues.

We aren't giving them the time, space, or strategies to truly invest in caring for themselves.

Teachers who recognize and name their emotions, understand their cause, and effectively regulate them are happier as humans and more comfortable as professionals. They are less likely to leave the profession due to job dissatisfaction or burnout. We know this, yet we still fail to provide teachers with the support they need to care for themselves.

Research presented by Tim Walker in a 2020 *NEA Today* article strongly suggests that incorporating social-emotional learning practices into teacher training programs helps teachers develop the skills to recognize and regulate their emotions effectively. SEL practices also help teachers foster positive relationships with their students, create a more positive classroom environment, and improve student outcomes.

However, despite the benefits of SEL practices, many teacher training programs fail to integrate them into their curriculum. Additionally, schools and districts may not prioritize SEL initiatives, leading to a lack of resources and support for teachers who want to incorporate these practices into their teaching.

Even more importantly, psychological safety is crucial for creating a supportive and inclusive work environment. Teachers who feel psychologically safe are more likely to share their ideas, collaborate with colleagues, and take risks in their teaching, leading to increased innovation and better student outcomes. However, many teachers report feeling unsupported and undervalued in their schools, leading to a lack of psychological safety. Feeling a lack of support can be particularly damaging for new teachers or those from marginalized communities who may already struggle to navigate the complex and often stressful world of teaching.

THE HACK: FOCUS ON WELL-BEING

We've all been there: it's Sunday night, and our hearts race as we combat the overwhelming feeling of anxiousness and the fear of checking our inbox. While the Sunday Scaries aren't isolated to the teaching profession, they are prevalent. Unfortunately for many teachers, Sunday is just pre-Monday, as they feel the need to grade papers, plan lessons, and answer the emails that have piled up since Friday afternoon. It's not that teachers don't love their jobs; it's that sometimes they live their jobs twenty-four-seven and don't give themselves the time or space to recover, rest, and rejuvenate.

Educational institutions must prioritize teachers' mental health and well-being and provide resources and support to help them manage stress and avoid burnout.

For our educators and staff to attend to the social-emotional needs of our students, we need to ensure we are responsive to their needs. First, be sure your staff is familiar with self-care practices to manage stress and emotions. Second, create a school environment that is conducive to practicing these skills.

Providing staff with access to resources and support for their mental health and well-being, such as counseling services and peer mentoring programs, creates a more supportive and inclusive workplace culture. By prioritizing their psychological safety, we help them build strong relationships with their students and colleagues, improve engagement and relational trust, and ultimately have a more significant impact on student learning.

In addition to promoting self-care practices among staff, it's essential that administrators provide them with the necessary resources and support to address students' social-emotional needs effectively. This might include professional development about trauma-informed care, restorative justice, and mindfulness practices. We can also create a culture that encourages open communication and collaboration among the staff so they can share their experiences and best practices for supporting students' social-emotional well-being.

If you were to ask teachers what they need to meet their social-emotional needs, their answers might surprise you. When we think of self-care, our minds often go to mindfulness and grounding exercises. However, here's what I found:

- Teachers want to be supported, be listened to, and not be micromanaged.

- They want to be told to go home at a reasonable hour.

- They don't like to receive emails at 1:00 a.m. that say, "See me in the morning."

- They want planning time in the school day so they don't have to write lessons on Sunday.

As administrators, we are responsible for creating conditions for teachers to feel supported from a social-emotional perspective. This involves helping them identify what they need for mental wellness and finding creative ways to make it happen. Our words must match our actions. We can't tell teachers we want them to care for themselves and then send a list of to-dos on a Friday. We can't tell our staff to unplug, then we turn around and send emails over the weekend with lists of tasks. And, yes, some of this is necessary. But some of it is not.

Self-care and social-emotional well-being are person-dependent. Teachers must communicate what they need, but leaders must also listen to them. What works for one won't work for another. The key is to support each teacher so that we may support all of them. It's hard, but it's also nonnegotiable.

WHAT YOU CAN DO TOMORROW

Supporting the social and emotional well-being of your teachers is an ongoing endeavor, but you can take steps to start tomorrow. And, just as important, be sure you are modeling self-care and taking steps to find a work-life balance for yourself.

- **Set a personal goal for self-care.** Just as a stressed teacher can't effectively care for students, depleted administrators can't effectively care for teachers. Make sure you are attending to your own self-care. What one thing can you commit to doing that will make a difference in your day? It may be granting yourself a short period of time to shut your door and eat lunch at school. It may be listening to your favorite music on the morning drive. Dig inside yourself for ways to care for your social-emotional well-being. Then commit to creating these habits and holding yourself accountable for following through. Sharing your goal with others is a wonderful way to keep yourself accountable. Tell your staff, friends, or family what you are doing and why. Taking care of yourself is undoubtedly a practice worth spreading and one that many of us can improve.

- **Model self-care.** School leaders are often not the best role models for self-care. We might tell teachers to pick a time to go home, but we stay until it's dark outside, neglecting dinner with our family or having fun with friends. We (I) need to be better at modeling self-care practices. Modeling what we hope to see isn't just good for teachers; it's good for us as well. Teachers need to see principals taking a lunch break. They need to see principals unapologetic about attending their child's soccer games. It seems simple, yet we don't often do it because we're afraid of what teachers will think if they see us leaving early. The reality is that if you've built trust, transparency, and understanding around self-care, you don't have to worry about what people think.

- **Listen.** Teachers will tell us what they are feeling, so we must be sure to listen. We can't just listen with our ears; we can also listen with our eyes. What is a teacher's body language telling us? Why are some teachers not eating lunch with their teams? Read the room. Build relational trust so teachers are open and honest about what they need. This only happens if we listen without judgment and don't try to fix the problem immediately. We need to truly understand what our teachers need right now and think strategically about how we can help them get it.

- **Acknowledge that mental health is health.** Mental health isn't just something we should do tomorrow; it's something we should have been doing yesterday. Unfortunately, the world has stigmatized mental health, making it hard to acknowledge and address. As a leader, we can recognize that mental health is no different than physical health. We can take it as seriously as the flu or a cold or virus. While mental health isn't contagious, it certainly won't get better if it's not prioritized.

A BLUEPRINT FOR FULL IMPLEMENTATION

Step 1: Assess current social-emotional needs.

Data is just as crucial for the adult community as it is for the student community. As leaders, we must be responsive to current realities rather than hunches. One way to know and understand these realities regarding adult mental health is to use an assessment tool to evaluate where teachers are in terms of their social-emotional well-being. This self-assessment doesn't necessarily need to be shared;

your staff can use it to identify areas of their strengths and challenges. They can use that data to set a targeted goal regarding their social-emotional learning, just as they do for professional learning and growth. Bringing awareness to our current mental health helps ensure the adults in the building are taking care of themselves. If they aren't caring for themselves, caring for students will be more difficult and maybe even impossible.

Acknowledge that mental health is health.

Whether you ask teachers to share their goals with you is up to you and, frankly, up to the teacher. There are a few benefits to knowing these goals. First, you can better know your teachers. Second, you can support teachers in the right ways at the right times. Also, there's a bit of accountability when sharing needs and goals. However, accountability doesn't mean compliance, and that's what it will turn into if you don't create an environment full of empathy, trust, and understanding.

Step 2: Prioritize setting boundaries.

Setting boundaries is essential to educators, and it's a staple of strong mental health. Without them, teachers are more susceptible to experiencing stress and burnout. Setting boundaries is challenging for teachers because many are perfectionists and want to meet the needs of students, even if it means giving too much of themselves. As an administrator, promote the idea that boundaries help teachers do better while being healthier.

We give time to what we believe is essential. Carving out time at the beginning of the year for teachers to define and establish boundaries is a good practice. Prioritizing time for staff to reflect on balancing their professional and personal lives shows that you are serious about teachers' social-emotional well-being.

Setting boundaries is an independent process. Your staff is in many different places, personally and professionally. What they can take on at any given time varies. Allow teachers to decide what feels comfortable to them right now; they can always reevaluate. If boundaries become mandates from the top down, they do more harm than good. Each person has a different way of communicating, organizing time, and defining availability. Your job is simply to support them as individuals as they make decisions about what they need.

Of course, you will likely have some general nonnegotiables, but it's most effective to give teachers freedom within those limits. For example, the nonnegotiable might be that teachers need to respond to families within twenty-four to forty-eight hours; the freedom is how they communicate. Some might prefer sending emails or using their cell phones, while others might only call from their work phones. Figure out where the line is, communicate that, and then allow teachers to decide how.

Step 3: Check in.

A weekly check-in is an efficient and effective tool for understanding where your teachers are regarding their social-emotional needs. It doesn't have to be lengthy or complicated. You can use a Google Form with two questions: "How do you feel going into this week?" and "What do you need from me to feel supported?"

This check-in helps you proactively meet the individual needs of your teachers, and it also allows you to see themes across the school. If a particular teacher is stressed, you may want to skip the evaluation planned for that teacher. If all your teachers feel they have a lot going on, consider how you can shift that feeling for the building; perhaps it's bringing in coffee or snacks or covering their recesses.

One great result of checking in with your staff is that it models an effective practice that teachers can emulate in their classrooms. Encouraging students to engage with one another before engaging in content builds psychological safety.

Step 4: Bring on the laughs.

Laughter is not just essential for students … adults need it, too. Laughter reduces stress and promotes well-being. It positively affects your body and brain by releasing dopamine, serotonin, and endorphins. Laughter is an excellent weapon against stress. Simply bringing humor into your school improves your school's culture and climate.

Now, I'm not saying you should stand up and tell jokes at your next staff meeting; trust me, nothing is funny at 4:00 p.m. However, find opportunities where you can incorporate humor in ways that feel comfortable to you as an individual. You can highlight kids' stories in your newsletter or show funny clips to kick off a professional development session. Perhaps you can identify staff members with a strong sense of humor and ask them to help bring some joy into the building. This is an excellent way to highlight a strength that sometimes goes unappreciated in a school. Also, kids are hilarious; have them tell jokes on the morning announcements. You can find countless ways to make humor happen.

Meeting students' needs is serious work, but it doesn't mean we always have to be serious. Using humor in tasteful, meaningful ways benefits everyone in your building, including you. Just use caution when it comes to sarcasm; some may see it as meanness with a smile. Keep humor to the ideas that uplift the community rather than put it down.

Step 5: Show you care.

Our actions speak volumes about what we find important. If our actions don't match our words in terms of self-care, teachers won't take our words seriously. Some of our best intentions get lost in the everyday business of the job. Below are examples of ways to show you care about the social-emotional well-being of your staff:

- When they call to tell you they're running late, tell them to drive safely.

- If they're sick, tell them to stay home to take care of themselves and text them to ask how they are doing.

- When they ask what they can wear, tell them whatever makes them happy.

- When they tell you their air conditioning isn't working, put the work order in immediately and check in on them until it's fixed.

- Take over their class if they ask you to leave a few minutes early for a doctor's appointment.

- When they tell you they have safety concerns, take them seriously and develop a plan to address them.

- Tell them to pick a time to leave in the evening and stick to it. Remind them the work will be there tomorrow.

The list could go on, and you have your own thoughtful ideas to add. Even the smallest gestures can mean a great deal.

OVERCOMING PUSHBACK

Perhaps the greatest barrier to teacher self-care is a lack of trust. For teachers to feel supported, take their concerns seriously. It's hard for teachers to admit they need help or support; when they do, we need to listen. Leaders can push back against the deficit narratives surrounding supporting mental health and well-being. Here are a few areas of pushback to anticipate and how to respond.

Teachers won't be honest. One of the greatest pushbacks I hear about doing an assessment or a check-in is that teachers won't be honest. There is some truth to this. Teachers won't be open in the absence of trust. Build that essential trust by working to meet their needs in nonjudgmental and authentic ways. If you become defensive when teachers advocate for themselves and what they need, they stop being open with you. But if you authentically listen with the intent of understanding and reflecting on a possible solution, they are more honest each time you ask. Teachers want to feel heard, and they want to trust their administrators. Trust doesn't magically happen; you have to be intentional about cultivating it.

> *Getting into classrooms rather than asking other staff members to step in speaks volumes about your care for your staff.*

We have a sub shortage. Teachers being absent certainly creates stress in the building, but it shouldn't get in the way of us encouraging teachers to take care of themselves. It certainly is frustrating when you don't have the staff you need; however, even when you feel stressed about coverage, you can extend human compassion to those who aren't there. It's harder for teachers to be absent than it is for them to show up sick or stressed. If you've ever made sub plans, you know this is true. We can't and shouldn't hold teachers accountable for the sub shortage. Instead, we need to think proactively about how we will cover when we don't have subs. Getting into classrooms rather than asking other staff members to step in speaks volumes about your care for your staff. While you may not always be able to do this, it's a valuable leadership move when you can.

They'll take advantage. When we extend freedoms about what teachers wear or allow them to leave early, there's always the worry that teachers will take advantage of the situation. This is rarely the case. And if it is, you handle it with that particular staff member rather than holding the whole staff accountable for the actions of a few. No one likes to receive a reprimand or have freedoms curtailed for something they didn't do.

They need to suck it up. I've heard leaders say this, and it saddens me. As educators, we know that without taking care of students' most basic needs, we can never reach their academic needs. This is also true of adults. We can't expect them to learn and grow and shift and change if we are constantly putting their needs on the back burner. Teachers need understanding. It's not easy to be present, but it's the right decision. Extend trust when people need to be anywhere other than school.

THE HACK IN ACTION

by Jody Ratti, educator

During and immediately following the COVID lockdown, caring for teachers became my primary concern. I reached out regularly until I found that the best way I could check in was to borrow an idea from CharacterStrong, an organization that provides resources and training programs to promote character development and social-emotional learning in schools. I sent out a regular check-in Google Form. It was brief and asked how teachers were doing, what was happening, and what I could do. My staff appreciated that I was reaching out, and even more so, they appreciated when I looped back with them and connected more personally.

I had multiple experienced teachers tell me that they had never had an administrator ask how they were doing in a meaningful way before, which both broke my heart for them and strengthened my resolve to show them the care they deserved.

Asking how someone was doing and then closing the loop with them when they needed something—anything—helped, but for many of my teachers, the simple fact that I was asking made a difference. I had staff share deeply personal concerns with me, while other staff members said they had no immediate concerns but knew that I was present for them ... and shared or vented later.

This established a standard for personal care for my teachers, many of whom then began to share the same level of care for their students. As with anything, modeling my actions and being explicit in my purpose helped teachers do the same with their students, which had an overall impact of improved attendance, engagement, and success. Students engaged in ways that teachers had not seen since before the pandemic shut schools down, and once students were engaged, personally or academically, everything started looking up. Staff started having a better year, discipline ticked down, and the overall vibe of the rooms improved. It created a positive upward spiral, and while it was hardly a panacea (these were some of the hardest years to be in education in my career), every minor improvement was a celebration.

We know that we need psychological safety to do our best work. Leaders can create spaces where teachers know their social-emotional well-being is prioritized. Teachers also need time to practice these skills. Building leaders can verify that their actions match their words when it comes to self-care by modeling self-care and by putting resources in teachers' hands so they can be their best selves.

Self-care is not a one-size-fits-all solution, and teachers have different needs and preferences when it comes to taking care of their mental health. Encourage them to explore self-care strategies, and provide a variety of resources that address their unique needs.

Another critical aspect of creating a psychologically safe environment is to promote open communication and feedback. Teachers should feel comfortable expressing their thoughts and concerns without fear of judgment or retaliation. Facilitate this by regularly soliciting feedback from teachers and taking concrete steps to address their concerns.

Finally, recognize that creating a balanced social-emotional environment is an ongoing process that requires continuous effort and investment. Prioritize the well-being of your teachers and make it a central part of your school culture. By doing so, you create a supportive and empowering environment that allows teachers to thrive and do their best work.

HACK 6

INVEST IN GROWTH
Harness the Power of Feedback

*Feedback is a gift only when it comes from
a person who has earned your trust.*
—GARY CHAPMAN, AUTHOR, SPEAKER, AND COUNSELOR

THE PROBLEM: OUR TEACHERS DON'T GET FEEDBACK

MANY TEACHERS CHOOSE a career in education with the intention of establishing safe environments where students can learn effectively. Some educators opt to become administrators to expand their impact and create a broader range of influence for the benefit of students. However, we also know that with the leadership role comes the responsibility to create safe spaces for our *adults* to continue learning and growing at high levels.

Instructional leadership is integral to being a principal, even if it doesn't feel like it right now. Teachers want to be the best they can be for their students, and they are doing their best with what they have. The principal's role as an instructional leader is to take what teachers are currently doing and work with them to take it to the next level. This is not a simple task. And—sadly—a lack of time and trust often gets in the way.

Feedback is essential to the growth process, yet our teachers often receive feedback only during the evaluation process. As a result, many teachers feel a sense of "I got ya" instead of "I've got you." The many demands of a school day have principals spending time away from the classrooms, but we can't let that happen. Principals need to work proactively to help teachers improve classroom management and instruction, or as a school, we will continue to work reactively, trying to fix kids instead of fixing our instruction.

Providing feedback to teachers is one of the most critical jobs of a principal. It's not enough to give feedback during the evaluation cycle; we need to provide meaningful, constructive comments frequently and in non-threatening ways. Remember that to grow students, we need to grow teachers. This won't happen if we don't make it happen.

Because administrators don't always give feedback at meaningful times and in meaningful ways, teachers don't value it as much as they would if administrators offered it more often and in ways that meant more than an arbitrary level given out of compliance during an evaluation. And if you're reading this believing that I'm judging, please know that I have also been the administrator running around in May with my computer. It's hard. Days are unpredictable, particularly in schools.

THE HACK: INVEST IN GROWTH

Investing in staff growth is one of our most high-leverage leadership moves. The very reason many of us became administrators was to widen our sphere of influence to meet the needs of more students. The way to do this is to invest in feedback and help our teachers grow. Teachers want to grow. Teachers want to be the best they can be for their students. That requires the intentionality and investment of leaders to help them grow, learn, and succeed.

> **Many teachers feel a sense of "I got ya" instead of "I've got you."**

Feedback is vital in building a productive and engaging learning environment because it builds trust, communication, and teamwork. It's not just about giving feedback; it's also the openness, vulnerability, and willingness to receive feedback. Although evaluation is inevitable and isn't going away (I can hear the crowd booing), additional feedback can happen outside of the evaluation process. Many teachers find this process threatening and redolent of compliance (and they are partly right), both of which break down the feeling of safety. When teachers don't feel safe, they can't focus on improvement. It's best if we provide feedback when teachers have their emotions in check and feel safe enough to take risks and motivated enough to try again. This isn't the typical mindset during the evaluation process, at least not in my experience.

Administrator feedback is best when it's timely and frequent. That said, for feedback to be meaningful, it also needs to be honest and sincere. Feedback should have a balance of authentic positivity and constructive criticism. Instead of just naming what needs to improve, offer guidance or suggestions on *how* to improve. Teachers want to know that their admin team believes in their success. By highlighting successes and connecting them to recommendations, we demonstrate our belief in teachers' abilities and provide them with tangible evidence of their impact. This recognition catalyzes further growth and encourages teachers to strive for even greater success.

Feedback doesn't have to come from administrators only. Teachers love getting into other teachers' rooms to share and receive feedback from people who don't evaluate them. Creating systems for peer feedback can be a welcome, non-stressful way to help teachers learn and grow. Not only does this benefit those receiving feedback, but it also helps the peers giving the feedback. It's a beautiful symbiotic relationship, and you're off the hook outside of its organization.

Regardless of where the feedback comes from, remember that not every teacher has the same entry point. Teachers are at many different places regarding their learning and comfort levels with criticism—positive or not. Knowing your teachers, clarifying their needs, and considering their openness and willingness to learn will serve everyone's best and highest interests.

WHAT YOU CAN DO TOMORROW

Investing in our teachers' growth begins with us. To grow others, we must be willing to look introspectively at our beliefs and actions to ensure we are ready and qualified to provide meaningful feedback to our staff. Our mindset when it comes to feedback needs to shift to seeing it as a tool for growth rather than for rating. When we make this shift, we are more likely to be sincere and honest with our feedback.

First, for teachers to see our comments as valuable, we need to make ourselves relevant in today's classrooms. Acknowledge who students are today rather than who they were five years ago. While children haven't necessarily changed, childhood has. Second, the effectiveness of our feedback is based on its delivery. That means using strength-based words and attributes. Third, we need to have trust. I might have said this five hundred times already, but it's worth saying five hundred more. Image 6.1 shows a quick and easy feedback form.

SEE, HEAR, IMPACT
FEEDBACK FOR:
WHAT I SAW...
WHAT IT SOUNDED LIKE...
HOW IT IMPACTS KIDS...

Image 6.1: Informal Teacher Feedback Form

And while the key to feedback is that it is ongoing, consistent, and timely, we can certainly find ways to get started on the right foot. Preparing our minds and words tomorrow will certainly help as we fully implement future feedback systems.

- **Change your mindset.** As educators, we know that formative assessment is equally important as summative assessment, if not more important. For some reason, we often forget this regarding feedback and evaluation. Perhaps it's because evaluation is required and feedback is suggested. A compliance factor is at play. It's essential to rewrite the narrative when it comes to feedback. See feedback as necessary for change and growth rather than just as an evaluation. I like to think that feedback is a comma while assessment is a period. They can coexist, but one is finite while the other emphasizes that there's more to come.

- **Get in classrooms.** If you want teachers to value your feedback, they need to see you as a teacher first. Many of us haven't been teachers for years. Therefore, we have a mental model of how kids used to be, not how they are. We need to get in front of students as much as possible for teachers to see us as teachers. This helps us better identify current needs and reflect on ideas to help meet them. We can't be effective instructional leaders if we aren't instructing. Being vulnerable by admitting that teaching is hard, even for someone leading a building, is comforting for teachers to hear. If we want our feedback to be well-received, we need to empathize with our teachers and their current realities. Getting into classrooms helps us remember how challenging and rewarding teaching is.

- **Drop "but," adopt "and."** When we are giving feedback, we often use a sandwich-like approach. We start with a positive comment, offer criticism, and then end with another positive. While this is an okay approach, it's also a bit predictable and canned. When we offer an affirmation, we follow it with the word "but." This word tends to negate the positive statement. Pay close attention to your word choice. Try replacing "but" with "and." The term "and" allows the recipient to digest the positive message and build on the suggestions. It's an easy, high-leverage way to offer constructive feedback.

A BLUEPRINT FOR FULL IMPLEMENTATION

Step 1: Build relational trust.

Relational trust is not an event; we build it slowly and consistently in the day-to-day interactions among the people in an organization. These interactions are based on a symbiotic relationship in which each upholds their responsibilities to the greater good. The role of the leader is to help define these responsibilities. Having a shared vision and mission and creating the conditions in which teachers can achieve them builds relational trust. These conditions include active listening, accepting vulnerabilities, and consistency. The most damaging action leaders can take is to build a culture in which staff don't know what to expect from them.

Your staff are likely doing their best. Getting to know them on a personal level, listening to them with the intent of understanding, and building a feeling of psychological safety all create relational trust.

If we are not intentional with building trust, feedback will continue to feel threatening. Know your staff so you can extend care and concern for each person while emphasizing that each individual is responsible for the success of the organization.

> *Your feedback takes teachers from good to great as long as you target the feedback to individuals and their specific situations.*

Step 2: Personalize feedback.

No universal template exists when it comes to feedback. The more we understand each individual teacher's strengths and challenges, the better we are at sharing comments that matter. Personalized feedback aligned to each teacher's area of need improves the chance of the teacher responding to the feedback. And the confidence that personalized feedback gives leads to greater competence and an even stronger level of trust between the administrator and staff. Note: Personalized feedback takes more time, so you may be giving it less often. However, it will be deeper and more meaningful.

> *For teachers:* We need to know how teachers prefer to receive feedback. Some teachers want it in writing, some prefer a face-to-face conversation, and others like input on the fly. An effective way of knowing what works best for each teacher is to ask them during conversations at the beginning of the year or as a warm-up question at a meeting.

> *For classes:* It's valuable to acknowledge the intricate dynamics of a class for which you are offering feedback. Teachers generally do not find it helpful when you are giving them feedback based on solutions you saw in another class or at another school. Teachers want to know what they can do better for their students in their class. Your feedback takes teachers from good to great as

long as you target the feedback to individuals and their specific situations.

Step 3: Be goal-oriented.

When it comes to receiving feedback, it's natural to feel a bit anxious and uncertain. That's where setting goals comes in. Here are a few practical steps:

1. Encourage teachers to set goals. This takes some guesswork and anxiety out of the feedback process and builds buy-in.

2. Provide feedback related to specific goals. Set by the teachers, these goals ensure the input is more targeted and focused and is more likely to yield the results they desire.

3. Be intentional about what you are looking for. Thus, the feedback is more objective, and data can often express the results.

4. Focus on *how* students are learning rather than solely on *what* they are doing.

5. Allow teachers to dictate what they want you to see. Setting goals creates the parameters for what they aim to achieve. This gives teachers a voice in the feedback process and makes it more meaningful and relevant to them.

Step 4: Use video to enhance feedback.

Teachers want to be part of the conversation to improve learning. Many times, we only see a snippet of what is happening in a classroom, so our feedback is based on some observations and inferences. We then fill the gaps in our knowledge with our own bias. When we create opportunities to bring reflection into the feedback process, we learn more about the intent and whether it matches the impact. One of the most powerful tools for providing feedback is using video to record the teacher's instruction, but only when you both decide on it together and you have established trust, since video can be intimidating. Watching the video allows teachers to think introspectively about their practice and identify their strengths and challenges. You then take on a coaching role to provide feedback for improvement. It might take time for teachers to get used to this, but it is an eye-opening and effective self-improvement exercise.

Step 5: Create systems for peer feedback.

Teachers have expressed frustration that administrators either have little classroom experience or that it wasn't recent. Sometimes, this means our feedback isn't as valuable as when it comes from those currently doing the work. Remember that we are not the only people who can improve instruction. We have a school full of experts committed to being lifelong learners.

Creating a culture of open communication and collaboration among your staff can bring about growth in a way that is more accepted by teachers. This does not mean the principal is absent from the feedback cycle. Instead, our role shifts to training teachers to give feedback effectively and providing clear guidelines and expectations for receiving feedback. In addition, principals support peer-to-peer feedback by allocating resources (such as time and management systems) so teachers can observe each other. This ties in beautifully with differentiated professional learning, allowing teachers to set goals and reflect on their own practice. Principals could potentially dedicate professional learning time to best practices for sharing feedback.

Principals facilitate peer-to-peer feedback in many ways. Classroom visits are a great example, as they are a highly effective and low-threat way to get teachers into other classrooms. Administrators, teachers, or other staff visit classrooms, observe instruction, and gather information about teaching and learning, usually around a specific goal or area of focus. The purpose is to provide insights into the classroom environment, identify strengths and challenges, and enhance best practices. Classroom visits are informal and outside of the evaluation system. You can facilitate this when you:

1. Collectively establish the purpose of the visits, generally around a school goal or initiative.

2. Develop a schedule and process for the visits, including who will go and what to look for.

3. Train teachers to deliver constructive feedback while maintaining confidentiality.

4. Gather data from the feedback, focusing on specific goals for specific action steps.

5. Use the data to help with whole-school learning.

OVERCOMING PUSHBACK

Teachers might not realize how much they value feedback since they usually only receive it when tied to a performance evaluation. Most teachers want feedback, but they want it from one another and from people they trust. Teachers certainly care what their administrators think ... as long as those administrators have an accurate story of what is happening in their classrooms. Here's some pushback you might encounter.

Teachers don't care what I think. Many principals believe their teachers don't care about feedback, so they don't fully grasp the importance of providing it in a timely and consistent way. Get into classrooms and do some teaching. This builds perspective and empathy for how it feels to teach students today rather than the ones you taught yesterday. Teachers do care what we think; they just don't want us to tell them what to do based on our time in the classroom ten years ago. They want relevant feedback on who they are and what they are trying to do. In addition, they don't always want our thoughts tied to their evaluations. They want to hear how we feel when we are focusing on improvement rather than on a rating.

There isn't time. We have tons of demands on our time, pulling us in various directions and leaving us overwhelmed and exhausted. Plenty of distractions keep us from getting into classrooms. However, our most important job as building leaders is to ensure students learn at high levels in a place where they feel they belong. If we aren't guiding the teachers to provide their students with these priorities, we are neglecting our number one responsibility as leaders.

We have to build our teachers' skill sets. Focusing on teacher growth ultimately benefits student learning. If you aren't proactive with feedback, you'll be reactive to challenging conversations. Many of your responsibilities can wait, but student learning can't. Do what you can to offer ongoing feedback in timely and consistent ways.

I already do this through evaluation. Formative assessment is about making the food, while summative assessment is about serving the food to guests. The same is true for feedback and evaluation. Evaluating comes with a sense of finality because it's typically tied to a rating. To assess teachers fairly, we need to provide feedback outside of the evaluation cycle so they have time to make changes and improve. Teachers want to know how they are doing toward accomplishing their goals in ways that are non-threatening and meaningful. Feedback yields more growth than evaluation ever will.

THE HACK IN ACTION

As an administrator, I was working with our first-grade team. Our collective group identified that our female students of color were underserved in math. It was heartbreaking to hear, but it was also an excellent opportunity for us to act and make a real difference in these students' lives.

We delved deeper into the issue and realized we needed more information about these students from an environmental, learner-specific, and instructional perspective. So, we worked together to build accurate stories about these students and their needs.

When it came time to understand the students from an instructional perspective, I knew we needed a different approach than just traditional evaluation. I suggested using introspective coaching and recording their math lessons to watch together as a team.

As we watched the videos, we asked questions and shared observations, and it was amazing to see how quickly the teachers became reflective practitioners. They recognized the instructional changes these students needed without me having to tell them. It was a powerful process that drew a clear line between feedback and evaluation.

And the best part? The teachers started seeking my feedback more frequently after that, and our work together built trust and created relationships I will always remember. It was incredible to see the contagious impact of our work and how teachers realized my job was to support them in becoming better, not just to judge them. It was a true honor to be part of that team and to watch those teachers grow and thrive.

But, most importantly, the impact on kids was significant. This group of students began excelling. They became engaged. They became learners ... simply because we made time for feedback.

To grow teachers, commit to giving them feedback that is timely, realistic, and consistent. For staff to embrace and use the feedback, build a culture of trust by being present, visiting classrooms, and structuring input centered on improvement and goals rather than on people. The best guidance not only improves the skills of the teachers but also benefits the students.

SERVE YOUR STAFF
Become a Servant Leader

*Servant leadership is all about making the goals
clear and then rolling your sleeves up and doing
whatever it takes to help people win. In that situation,
they don't work for you; you work for them.*
—KEN BLANCHARD, BUSINESS CONSULTANT, AUTHOR, AND SPEAKER

THE PROBLEM: COMPLIANCE IS THE FOCUS

WE ARE LOSING teachers in large numbers due to the demands placed on them. I know I keep saying this, but it's important. We need teachers. We need to find ways to attract and retain them by building safe and productive cultures and climates within the walls of our schools. Unfortunately, hierarchical structures such as those present in traditional leadership create cultures of compliance over empowerment. In these top-heavy structures, teachers end up stressed and dissatisfied.

The title of principal creates a power imbalance between us and those we serve … unless we work diligently against that stigma.

The very definition of leadership is about responsibility and power, leading to the hierarchical structure that now needs dismantling. Sometimes we get stuck behind our titles, making mandates, policies, and procedures without helping the people around us grow as leaders.

While this can be efficient, it isn't effective.

When we force compliance and rigid rules within an educational setting, we inadvertently foster a culture and climate that heavily relies on individual personalities rather than systemic processes. This person-dependent culture becomes a barrier to replicating success when there is a lack of or change in leadership. When you implement a systems-based, people-centric approach, success becomes more replicable and sustainable. The emphasis shifts from individual efforts to collaborative and collective responsibility. The system itself becomes a source of stability and support, enabling teachers and other stakeholders to thrive and contribute to the overall success of the school, even in the absence of the leader.

THE HACK: SERVE YOUR STAFF

To create a people-centered environment, we need to put our staff first. That means embracing humility, building relationships, and choosing to improve our culture and climate over policies, procedures, ratings, or rankings. We do not reinforce our power but rather focus on empowering those in our care, build on their strengths, and intentionally improve our culture and climate.

The role of the principal has changed over the last few years. Teachers once leaned on the building leader's authority to drive the school's direction and ensure follow-through. In recent years, we've seen a growing desire for leaders to build a collective vision and an even stronger desire for principals to put their staff before themselves. Most teachers want a servant leader over a traditional leader, even if they don't specifically name it. A servant leader is people-centric and works to understand the needs and wants of others. In addition, servant leaders remove the barriers in the way of those needs and wants.

> *Having a principal who is a servant leader sets the tone for the entire school and creates a supportive culture that benefits all stakeholders.*

Now more than ever, we need to improve the social-emotional health of our staff. Servant leadership emphasizes learning, well-being, and empowerment that create an atmosphere of trust, efficacy, growth, and inclusion. These are qualities teachers are looking for in their school culture. Teachers want to know they are working for someone looking out for their best interests. They want to feel seen, heard, valued, and trusted. Servant leadership is more likely to produce these results than traditional leadership.

In this model, the leader holds power in title only. A servant leader's actions center on humility, empowerment, and encouragement. This is not to say that, as leaders, we are absent of authority. It means using that authority to put people first, which makes a positive difference. It isn't just the staff who benefit. Leaders benefit as well, establishing more significant commitment and engagement, ultimately improving the school's productivity and success. And all of this benefits our kids.

Having a principal who is a servant leader sets the tone for the entire school and creates a supportive culture that benefits all stakeholders. Servant leadership focuses on collaboration, empathy, and personal growth to build trust and foster a sense of community, which is needed in today's landscape. By putting the needs of others first, a servant leader principal can create a safe, inclusive, and motivating environment that encourages innovation. This is an effective way for the principal to develop strong relationships with staff and students, create a sense of shared purpose, and promote positive outcomes for the entire school community. And who doesn't want that?

WHAT YOU CAN DO TOMORROW

Start tomorrow and implement steps to pave the way for your role as a servant leader. Begin with self-reflection, shifting the dynamic from "me" to "we" … and you can start now. If you want to attract and retain teachers, you need to get started.

- **Self-reflect.** To be a servant leader, first understand who you are and what you believe is important. Define your goals and motivations and recognize what is standing in your way. Self-reflection also shows you how your vision aligns with your community's collective vision. All this leads to better trust, listening, empowerment, and stewardship.

- **Think like a teacher.** Empathize with your teachers by better understanding what they might require in certain situations. The greater your ability to view their decisions from their perspective, the more significantly you can serve teachers by removing the barriers that hinder their goals. Approach every decision you make with empathy and support. This isn't easy, as some of us have been out of the classroom for a while. You might need to seek guidance from other teachers. This is a more complex process; however, even as soon as tomorrow, you can ask yourself to remember what it's like being a classroom teacher. This reflection can guide you in your next steps.

- **Add value.** Start each day by asking what you can do to add value to the day. Staying in touch with day-to-day happenings helps you determine where the gaps are and where your service is most valuable. For example, if you're short on people for lunch duty, get in the cafeteria and help. If your custodial department is understaffed, ask how you might help them for the day. Each day, you have the opportunity to add value to your staff and school; strive to fill the gaps with consistency and intentionality.

A BLUEPRINT FOR FULL IMPLEMENTATION

Step 1: Build community.

Becoming a servant leader begins with building a strong community. Work hard to know your staff and understand their strengths and challenges. Find out who your team is and what they need to feel safe through one-on-one conversations or a survey with one weekly question. Offer opportunities for staff to get to know one another, establishing relationships that encourage more buy-in and engagement in the work you are doing together and creating a sense of belonging.

We build community by centering our work on a common goal to do our best for all students. This shared focus helps teams remain consistent on the *why* even when they disagree on the *how*.

Step 2: Communicate.

Be on the lookout for opportunities to communicate with your staff in positive ways. This means being in classrooms, the hallway, the lunchroom, and the parking lot. Building a foundation of goodwill makes it easier in the future when you navigate hard conversations or seek input. Remember that what you do and say set the tone for your entire school and staff. Here are six communication tactics to create goodwill and build trust:

1. Schedule one-on-one meetings with all staff members to get to know them better. Use this time to build rapport and establish trust.

2. Conduct a survey with one weekly question to gauge staff members' needs and interests. Staff can complete the survey anonymously to encourage honest responses.

3. Organize team-building activities such as a staff retreat, games, or social events outside of work hours. Encourage participation and make sure everyone feels included.

4. Develop a collective goal focused on doing your best work for all students. Involve staff members in creating this goal to ensure buy-in and ownership.

5. Be visible and available to staff members by being present in classrooms, hallways, and common areas. Use the interactions to communicate positively and build relationships.

6. Model the behavior you want to see from staff and students. Be respectful, honest, and transparent in your communication and actions.

Step 3: Listen, then act.

Listening is vital to becoming a servant leader. Not only do we need to listen, but we also need to listen well. We must understand what our staff needs to successfully meet their own and their students' social, emotional, and academic needs. Once we understand these needs, we can respond in ways that make this goal attainable.

Often, we are listening with the intent to reply (I'm totally guilty). This type of listening puts us and our needs at the center. Instead, listen to figure out what you can do to serve your staff in meaningful ways, including removing barriers. It's easy to get distracted when we are in the process of listening. These distractions may communicate that whatever is happening outside the conversation is more important than the person you are speaking with. It's crucial to remove these distractions.

It's also essential that this listening process leads to intentional action. If teachers are telling you it's a busy time of year, listen to their ideas about what to remove to create realistic expectations, and then do all you can to eliminate the non-priorities.

Step 4: Be a visionary.

Actually, be more than a visionary ... form grand ideas about your school's future. This can be challenging for a principal as we tend to focus on day-to-day operations. While knowing what is happening in the present is essential for a leader, it's also important to gain a bigger perspective and keep it in our heads as we make daily decisions.

Dreaming big is a task for your whole team, not just you. A collective vision inspires people to understand the rationale behind immediate decisions. A good strategy to make this happen is a vision board, which provides visual support for staff to keep the vision in the forefront, even with daily interruptions.

We recognize that these interruptions are also integral to our work. We acknowledge that the immediate decisions made during these interruptions significantly influence our overarching vision.

Step 5: Empower your team.

Empowering your people creates opportunities for shared leadership as you acknowledge that others add value to the organization. It means putting collective goals before individual ones.

Your job in empowering others is to cheer on your staff and support their needs appropriately, showing them that this isn't about you and your leadership but rather about them and what they bring to the organization. Showing humility is a key tenet of servant leadership. Admitting that you might not be the expert or the best person for a job models fallibility and allows others to see your vulnerability.

This might include asking staff members to lead professional learning, chair a committee, or serve on the PTO. You have countless ways to include others. Most people want to step up ... as long as they know their leader supports them.

Step 6: Take the fall.

Sometimes, life doesn't go as planned. It's easy to point fingers. But true leadership means looking introspectively and taking the fall for the staff. This is a true act of servant leadership and reflects selflessness and accountability. When leaders take responsibility for decisions that don't yield the desired outcomes, they set an example that can deeply resonate with their team members. By willingly accepting the blame when needed, leaders create an environment where individuals feel safe to take risks and explore new possibilities, which is essential for organizational growth and innovation.

Taking the fall also reinforces trust and respect within the team. This act of humility and vulnerability fosters an environment where open communication, collaboration, and learning thrive. It encourages team members to take ownership of their actions, learn from their mistakes, and strive to be better.

True success lies in the success of those you serve. Your personal accomplishments are not the sole measure of achievement. Instead, the ability of your team, such as teachers, to meet students' academic and social-emotional needs determines your effectiveness. If this is not occurring, reflect inwardly and explore how to support teachers in better ways.

> **By willingly accepting the blame when needed, leaders create an environment where individuals feel safe to take risks and explore new possibilities.**

Step 7: Share the wins.

Sharing praise with your staff and giving credit to others for their achievements fosters a positive and supportive work environment. When families take the time to express gratitude for the actions of individual staff members or the collective team, it clearly indicates that your staff is making a positive impact and the school is achieving success. Recognizing and celebrating these wins is vital to maintaining morale and motivation among your staff. Check out Image 7.1, which you can create as a staff survey.

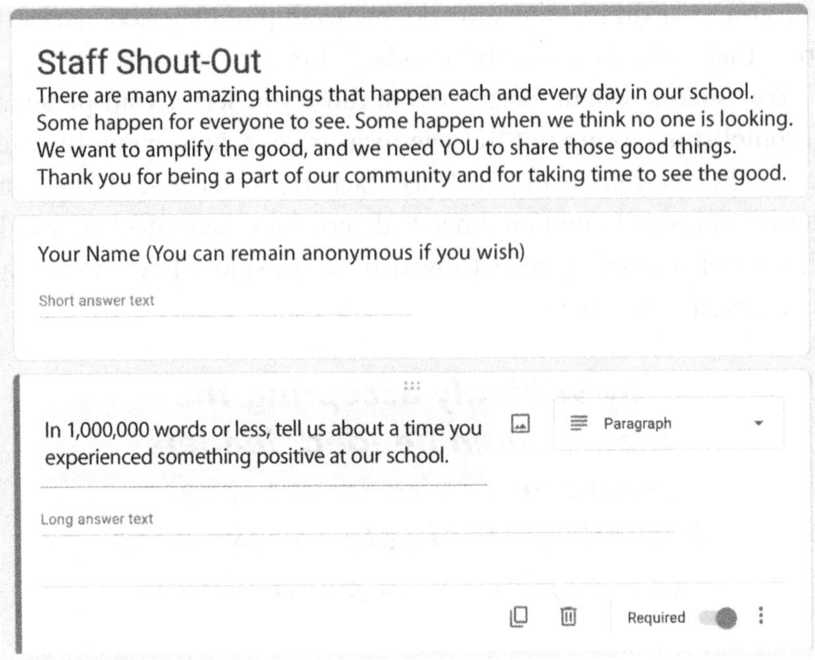

Staff Shout-Out

There are many amazing things that happen each and every day in our school. Some happen for everyone to see. Some happen when we think no one is looking. We want to amplify the good, and we need YOU to share those good things. Thank you for being a part of our community and for taking time to see the good.

Your Name (You can remain anonymous if you wish)

Short answer text

In 1,000,000 words or less, tell us about a time you experienced something positive at our school.

≡ Paragraph

Long answer text

Required

Image 7.1

Acknowledging and appreciating the efforts and accomplishments of your staff helps them feel valued and recognized for their hard work. When you receive emails or thank you notes from families or other stakeholders, ensure the praise reaches the hands of the staff involved. Sharing these messages of appreciation boosts the morale of the individuals being praised and creates a culture of recognition and support within the school community. You can share these messages in various ways, such as forwarding emails, creating a dedicated space to display positive feedback, posting in secure and private digital communication boards, and sharing them out loud to kick off staff meetings.

Internal recognition is another key to a servant leadership culture. Encourage your staff members to appreciate and acknowledge each other's achievements and contributions. Creating opportunities for peer-to-peer recognition, such as staff shout-outs during meetings or establishing a recognition program, can further enhance the sense of camaraderie and support within the school community.

Sharing the wins highlights how individual accomplishments contribute to the greater community. It also makes it much easier for people to focus on what is going right rather than on what is going wrong. And while it feels good when people acknowledge us and give us credit as leaders, it feels even more rewarding to share that acknowledgment and credit.

Step 8: Seek feedback.

You already know that feedback is vital (Hack 6 is all about it). Specifically, feedback as it pertains to servant leadership is a way to improve awareness and foresight. Recognize how your words and actions affect those around you and practice having the humility and courage to correct your mistakes, even if you spent a long time making them.

Feedback helps you stay attuned to your school. It allows you to understand how people are truly feeling and what you need to do to support each one. This may mean pushing aside your opinion of how things are going so you can acknowledge the lived experiences of your teachers and other staff.

Using feedback, whether written or verbal, to create plans is a way of being responsive and having foresight. Foresight allows you to use past experiences and mistakes in combination with current realities to help you and your team make decisions regarding the future. It bears repeating that the feedback you seek should be rooted in openness and honesty instead of coercion or control. This can only happen in an environment where you have established trust and sincere communication.

OVERCOMING PUSHBACK

Like all leadership models, servant leadership is not without challenges or pushback. It can lead to empathy fatigue and doesn't fit into every situation. You still need to rely on authority and management at times and to hold teachers accountable. You may encounter the following three arguments most often.

Servant leadership impacts authority. Authority still lies with the leader; how you use that authority transforms traditional leadership into servant leadership. Rather than putting yourself first, acknowledge the current realities while promoting a collective vision. Put the good of your team and your school first. Use your authority to listen and empower and then support and encourage the team's strengths, voices, and ideas.

I need to manage. While there will always be managerial aspects to leadership, servant leadership changes your management focus to the team's needs. Rather than managing everything, use empowerment and stewardship to delegate responsibility and leadership. Identify the gaps in the greater organization and help your team address them. Your role is not to lead the charge but rather to encourage your teachers and staff and to remove the barriers that hinder their success. We are still managers; it is what we are managing that changes.

There's no accountability. As leaders, we certainly need to hold people accountable. Often, however, accountability leads to compliance—ensuring that people did what they were supposed to do in the way they were supposed to do it. Instead, accountability in servant leadership is not about dropping those high expectations but rather giving your staff the trust and freedom to accomplish a task and understanding why a person chose to do a job in a specific way. It's about encouraging risk-taking, mistake-making, and creative problem-solving, even if it differs from what we had in our minds. Allow people to be who they are without compromise. Thus, accountability is more about moving toward the collective goal and less about how we move forward.

THE HACK IN ACTION

As a principal, I know that taking the fall for mistakes is one of the most significant acts of leadership. Each year, our school hosts a Passport Night. This is an event in which we highlight the different cultures in the school by creating displays. Families provide information, demonstrations, artifacts, and food to teach others about their culture. One day, we received a phone call from a family. It turned out we had scheduled Passport Night during Ramadan. This caused both confusion and frustration about our mission. It would have been easy to pass the blame since this is an event planned by our Parent Teacher Organization.

At the end of the day, though, I was the person who ultimately approved the date. And I was the person who needed to look out for, respect, and represent each of our kids. Thus, it was my job as the school leader to take responsibility for the mistake. I sent out the following email to our community:

Families,

One of the most important messages we teach our students is that much of our learning comes from mistakes. It isn't the actual making of mistakes but rather the fixing.

Passport Night typically takes place earlier in the year; however, at its regularly scheduled time, we weren't able to meet in person, so we postponed. Once we learned we were able to have in-person events, I quickly searched for a date for one of our most beloved events. In doing so, however, I overlooked Ramadan. In hosting this event at our original date, we would be excluding some of our families from participation, which is the opposite of our intentions and certainly the antithesis of Passport Night. I am sorry for this oversight.

As a result, Passport Night will take place on May 12th from 6–8 p.m. Please see the attached flyer for updated information.

The most important way to improve our cultural competence is to honor lived experiences and perspectives. If ever we overlook something like this, don't hesitate to reach out and let us know. When we know better, we do better. At Green Trails, we want each of us to feel like we belong without having to compromise who we are. I own the mistake, and hope that you all will be available to celebrate on the new date!

Thank you all so much for helping us be the amazing community we are.

The responses to my email showed that the community appreciated my humility and ownership. The event was a huge success, and when it came time to give praise for the event, I extended it to those around me. Not only is it my job to take the fall but also to give the praise.

Serving your staff is integral to a healthy organization. Leading by concentrating on others instead of on yourself is the heart of servant leadership. Being a servant leader does not remove your authority but shifts how you use it, focusing less on compliance and more on encouragement, empowerment, and multiplying leadership. Instead of looking at how you will benefit, look at how you can help others through an act of service. This builds a solid foundation for your relationship with your team and works toward a successful collective vision.

As the world continues to adapt to the impact of the pandemic, it is important for leaders to adopt an approach that prioritizes the growth and well-being of staff. Servant leadership embodies the growing trend toward a more caring leadership model that both grows staff and brings them happiness. By creating a supportive learning environment, leaders foster a culture of trust and collaboration, ultimately leading to happiness and better outcomes for students.

While servant leadership is not without challenges, the benefits outweigh the costs. Acknowledge how traditional leadership structures fit into servant leadership and decide what adjustments you can make to create a people-centered organization through service.

HACK 8

MINIMIZE DISTRACTIONS
It's Always a Great Day to Be a Principal

Less distraction, more focus. Less gossip, more encouragement.
Less past, more future. Less toxicity, more positivity.
—Robin Sharma, Canadian writer

THE PROBLEM: TEACHERS CAN'T ACCESS THEIR WHY

WHEN YOU ASK teachers what they want from a principal, many tell you they wish for someone who removes barriers and distractions so they can help students learn at high levels. Many distractions pop up within the school day; unfortunately, the principal can be one of them. This might not be intentional, but failing to act as a filter for these interruptions can harm the classroom environment.

Angry parents, student dysregulation, state legislation, and standardized test scores are inherent time and attention demands. As a principal, we can't make these realities disappear, but how we respond to them certainly impacts how our teachers respond in turn. Often, we let them affect our daily operations and, as a result, negatively impact instruction. This frustrates our teachers and leads to stress, fatigue, and burnout as they try to respond to these demands and still provide high levels of instruction.

Our teachers want nothing more than to meet the needs of our students socially, emotionally, and academically. They need a principal who can filter so they can do what they came to do. Teachers are aware of their why. They need a leader who removes the barriers that are getting in the way of it.

THE HACK: MINIMIZE DISTRACTIONS

What we say, how we say it, and how we act set the tone for the entire building. If we use a deficit-based approach or complain about behavior in non-constructive ways, our teachers feel it and ultimately believe it themselves. Our role as a principal is to be the filter. We need to control the overall message and ensure our teachers have what they need to do what they want to do most— meet the needs of their students.

One key to honoring teachers is to recognize the significance of minimizing distractions in their professional lives. Distractions can come in various forms, such as excessive administrative tasks, interruptions during instructional time, or nonessential meetings. We are responsible for acting as filters, carefully considering what should be allowed to reach teachers and when. This involves being selective in the information and requests we pass on to teachers, ensuring they have the time and resources to carry out their core responsibilities effectively.

To be a leader who centers our teachers and staff, we need to prioritize the well-being and professional growth of those we serve. This means being vigilant in managing the flow of information and requests, shielding teachers from unnecessary distractions, and creating a balanced workload. This does not mean isolating teachers from everything but carefully evaluating the value and impact of each potential distraction before allowing it to enter the teachers' domain and prioritizing the information and opportunities that align with our collective goals.

Filter yourself.
Filter the barriers.
Filter the demands.

Our job as a filter is to control what gets in and remove unwanted ingredients ... the distractions that take teachers away from meeting the needs of their students.

Filter yourself

Teachers have enough to do without us placing our own struggles on them. As a principal, your attitude toward distractions shapes how teachers view them. If you come back from a meeting saying that meetings are a waste of time, you set yourself up for your teachers to feel the same way. Be sure that what you say and how you say it doesn't add to your teachers' stress. You can still show feelings and express when you are not thrilled with a decision. However, it's best to find job-alikes or other trusted people outside the organization and express those feelings to them without bringing your vent session into the building.

Filter the barriers

Teachers don't need us to remind them of their why. It is and always will be related to their kids. As leaders, we need to know what is getting in the way of their ability to access their why. And then we need to respond, removing the barriers that prevent teachers from meeting their students' needs. This can be challenging, as many tasks we ask of teachers did not originate in our office, but our attitude and words, and how we roll out the tasks, make a difference. This isn't just about initiative overload. This is about ensuring that we know our staff, implement the best plan for them, and prioritize what is necessary.

Filter the demands

Remember what it was like to be a teacher. Reflecting on our experiences as educators allows us to empathize with the challenges and responsibilities that teachers face daily. Then, we can do better at respecting their time, trust, and workload.

WHAT YOU CAN DO TOMORROW

Our immediate and long-term behaviors set the tone for the building. What we say, how we say it, and how we behave impact what our teachers say, how they say it, and how they behave. Our role as leaders is to ensure we only let in what we hope to see and replicate. While being the buffer is an ongoing process, we can take steps immediately to help our staff meet the needs of their students.

- **Start positive, end positive.** If you want your staff to do their best, foster a positive work environment. Minimizing distractions and eliminating toxicity create the conditions for your staff to access their why. Look for possibilities and positive outcomes instead of barriers and failures. Be realistic, but be sure you aren't perpetuating negativity in your actions. It's okay to embrace the yuck with your staff occasionally; however, as a leader, you need to reframe the yuck into possibilities. This isn't easy, but it's worth it. One way to do this is to end with a positive. It doesn't matter if it's a staff meeting, daily announcement, or email. Pointing out what is going well and how it impacts students builds a positive narrative that, in turn, uplifts everything you try to do as a school and a team.

- **Check your face.** Do your facial expressions match the emotions you're trying to convey? In many ways, our expressions communicate more than our words. The COVID-19 pandemic certainly helped us realize that. We lost the ability to see smiles and frowns, which many rely on to read emotions. And while almost anyone can fake a smile, we express genuine emotion in our eyes and our brows. While it may take more than a day to train your face to convey a feeling of openness and trustworthiness, what you can do tomorrow is pay attention to what your face is saying at different parts of the day. Are your eyes alert? Open? Is your brow furrowed? Is your face worried, stressed, or disappointed? If so, your staff will know, regardless of what your words tell them. These nonverbal cues significantly impact your message. If you want to be believable when trying to be positive, ensure that your facial expressions match your sentiments.

- **Rephrase it.** Coining a catchphrase is a great way to keep a positive culture and filter out negativity. A shared saying can help you realign the current reality to your collective mission, even when it feels like your world is falling apart. This prevents leaders from laying stress on their staff, who aren't in control of the situation anyway. Using a catchphrase might seem shallow or cheesy, but it can also be a mood-shifter. When I think of the purpose of a catchphrase, I am reminded of the scene in *Titanic* where the ship is sinking but the orchestra is peacefully playing on the deck despite the emergency. A catchphrase can be a way of telling your staff that no matter what is happening, you're going to be all right.

You don't need to create something new. Use your school mascot as an easy anchor. For example, if you are the Gators, you might say, "It's a great day to be a Gator." Catchphrases should be short, representative, and easily shared. Even at the most stressful times, when someone asks you how you are, you can use this statement. Even if it's not true right then and there, it will remind you and those with whom you interact that everything will be okay.

A BLUEPRINT FOR FULL IMPLEMENTATION

Step 1: Figure out what is distracting and remove it.

One way to filter out what is unwanted or unnecessary is to ask your staff for suggestions about what to cut. Because your view from the big seat doesn't often give you the same perspective as teachers, it's essential to ask them. Leaders can do this weekly, monthly, or quarterly. Image 8.1 shows three simple questions that can help you make sound decisions as a leader regarding what you might filter out or modify.

QUARTERLY CHECK-IN

NAME:

FIST-TO-FIVE: HOW IS YOUR STRESS?

0   1   2   3   4   5

WHAT ARE YOU HOPING TO ACCOMPLISH THIS QUARTER?

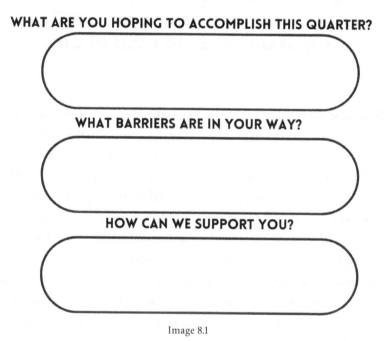

WHAT BARRIERS ARE IN YOUR WAY?

HOW CAN WE SUPPORT YOU?

Image 8.1

These barriers might include administrative tasks, time constraints, lack of professional development, high workload, or student behavior. Look at these barriers individually or systemically. If you want to minimize distractions, you need to know what you should be letting through to your staff and what you shouldn't.

Step 2: Filter out difficult caregivers.

Parents and caregivers are an integral part of the school community. We want them to feel they belong within our buildings. That said, these relationships can be a challenging aspect of an educator's job. It's not necessarily *what* caregivers are advocating for; most of the time, we agree. Sometimes it's *how* they advocate that can add stress and pressure on school staff, particularly teachers.

> **One way to filter out what is unwanted or unnecessary is to ask your staff for suggestions about what to cut.**

Building relationships with our families is an essential step in supporting our staff. The more goodwill and trust we build with families, the better the outcome will be when we back our team and their decisions. On the flip side, we are also responsible for keeping the trust between teachers and families. When we get an email from a caregiver, our first question should be, "Did you talk to the teacher?" We can avoid or solve so much conflict simply by encouraging people to speak to one another.

Being the filter for angry parents and caregivers means listening to them and the teacher without judgment. It means being responsive to your teachers' needs and understanding the role they want you to play with individual families.

In addition, you must establish trust with families. Start by calling five to ten parents or caregivers each week. Check in. Share positive information. This trust and goodwill will go a long way in supporting your teachers. Is it time-consuming? Yes. However, what you build in the beginning will save you time when issues arise. One caveat, however, is to make sure you aren't pulling away the families' trust in teachers and staff. This is, again, where those relationships and trust will pay off.

Step 3: Help with student behavior.

If you ask teachers what they would most like support with, you will likely hear them say student behavior. Teachers spend a significant portion of their time addressing it. The more efficient and effective your practices are regarding discipline, the more distractions you eliminate (see the book *Hacking School Discipline* for guidance). To do this, create clear guidelines regarding what should be handled in class and what should be handled in the office. In addition, clearly define acceptable consequences to help teachers know what to do at the moment. If you use a form, be sure the information required is specific and not overwhelming.

It's also imperative to provide professional learning opportunities about school discipline, particularly for new teachers and support staff. This should involve strategies for communicating with individuals from diverse cultural and linguistic backgrounds and ways to respond to students with substantive health needs. While providing professional learning seems like more work, it's a way of frontloading so we protect time and avoid misunderstandings in the long run.

While we can never truly shield our teachers from having to address discipline, our proactive efforts and general support will save them time when they know what to do in each situation.

Step 4: Stay asset-based.

Being the principal means having the power to influence the attitudes and behaviors of others. When we approach situations from a positive perspective, we build trust with our staff and create safe conditions for change. Being asset-based means focusing on strengths and potential. This attitude minimizes the distractions and limitations of negativity and focuses on the solution.

One way to stay asset-based is to celebrate your realities positively. When you celebrate where you are versus where you started, even if you've only taken small steps, you build momentum toward shared goals and don't waste time on negativity.

Another method is to ground your meetings in an accountability statement. This is a statement you use with one another to focus conversations on the goal. It's important to teachers because time is at a premium. For example, I ask teachers to anchor our discussion with "To what degree does this conversation support belonging for this student and all students?" Using a centering statement minimizes wasted time caused by fixating on the problem.

Step 5: Remain consistent.

By being consistent, leaders create an environment that minimizes distractions and allows team members to concentrate on their tasks effectively. People are more likely to trust and follow us when they know what to expect. Inconsistency leads to uncertainty and creates an organization where people waste time waiting for the other shoe to drop. We remain consistent when we:

- stay grounded in what matters
- check in with our people
- self-reflect
- ensure our actions match our words

Consistency in leadership minimizes distractions by providing clarity, predictability, and stability for the team. When your team understands what to expect and why you made certain decisions, they can focus on finding solutions and achieving their goals rather than on wasting time speculating about the leader's next move. While people might not always like what you have to say or what you do, they will know why you are doing it. This reduces pushback, increases trust, and allows the team to work more efficiently toward their collective objectives. Image 8.2 shows another survey I consistently send out to see how people are doing.

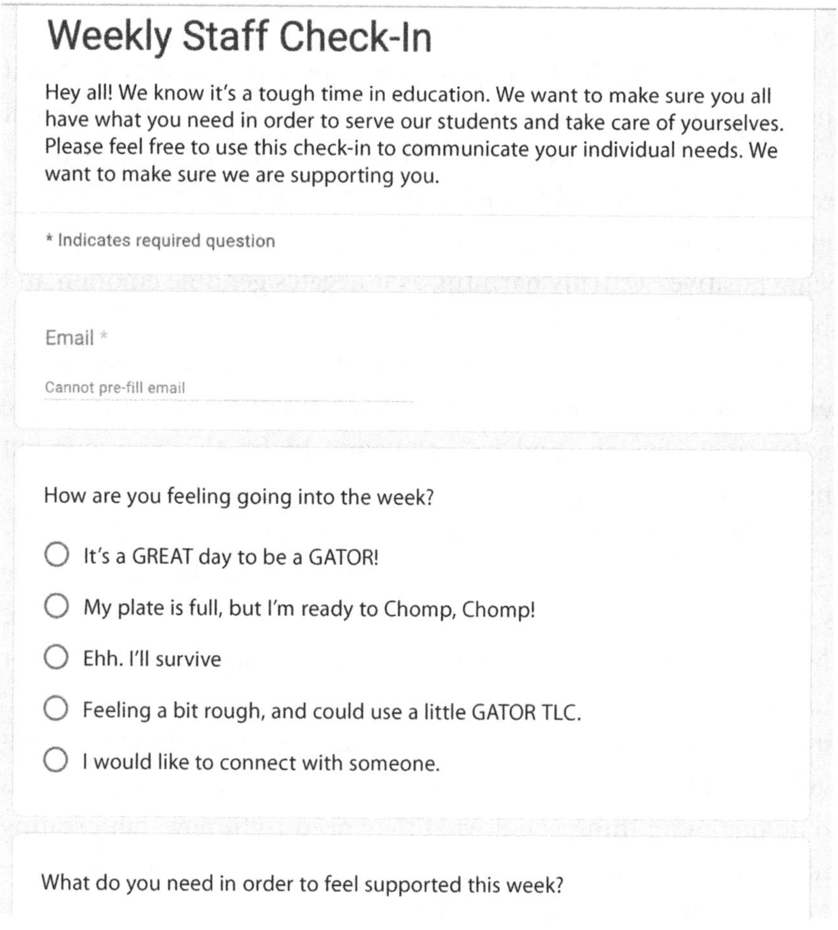

Weekly Staff Check-In

Hey all! We know it's a tough time in education. We want to make sure you all have what you need in order to serve our students and take care of yourselves. Please feel free to use this check-in to communicate your individual needs. We want to make sure we are supporting you.

* Indicates required question

Email *

Cannot pre-fill email

How are you feeling going into the week?

○ It's a GREAT day to be a GATOR!

○ My plate is full, but I'm ready to Chomp, Chomp!

○ Ehh. I'll survive

○ Feeling a bit rough, and could use a little GATOR TLC.

○ I would like to connect with someone.

What do you need in order to feel supported this week?

Image 8.2

OVERCOMING PUSHBACK

Leaders and educators may face pushback when implementing asset-based practices in their schools due to concerns about toxic positivity, mandates, and the perceived insincerity of this approach. Acknowledge these concerns and work toward implementing authentic and effective practices that support the well-being and success of all your students and staff. Here are examples of push-back you may hear when you work to minimize distractions for your team.

Positivity must be toxic positivity. Some people may fear that these steps will lead to toxic positivity. However, they are different concepts with different actions. Toxic positivity is a real fear for leaders and teachers alike and is rooted in the idea that no matter how grim or devastating a situation is, we can fix it simply by being positive. It's truly harmful, as it negates genuine emotion and shames people for having these feelings.

However, we also want to ensure that we continue to move forward, even slowly. We overcome toxic positivity by allowing people to feel their feelings and by not trying to fix the emotions but instead focusing on the problem and potential solutions.

It looks like we're ignoring the mandates. We can't free ourselves from mandates; we must navigate outside demands. While we can't always choose what those mandates are, how we present them makes a difference. When a decision comes from the state or district level, minimize the distraction it might cause by making it fit with what you are already trying to achieve. Familiarize yourself with that mandate enough to make it your own. Asking teachers to do one more thing is not what they need right now, but creating more favorable conditions for them to accept a mandate will make it one less distraction for your team.

Teachers will see through this. You're right. When teachers hear your catchphrase, they may realize you are covering up for a problematic or negative situation. But what they will also realize is that you are filtering out what's problematic or negative. As long as you have their trust, they will appreciate this. Filtering out distractions will be a welcome relief to teachers as long as you are transparent about what they need to know.

Teachers won't understand. It's true that teachers may not fully understand the process or rationale for minimizing distractions. As a result, they may push back, feeling as though it is taking away from their individuality or flexibility within the classroom. Remain transparent regarding the process and purpose of minimizing distractions. Once again, it's about trust and communication.

THE HACK IN ACTION

Teachers' workloads are significant, and unfortunately, we don't always have control over how we can lighten the load. I know I have been guilty of making assumptions about what and how. Experience has taught me that I'm no longer the best person to decide what is distracting teachers ... we simply need to ask them.

I remember a time when we introduced our teachers to new legislation about literacy. You could practically feel the air getting sucked out of the room. It was obvious they were overwhelmed. However, legislation is legislation, and that is a place where I don't have much control. I knew there *were* areas where I could decide what no longer felt important; I just wasn't sure *what* they were.

To make an informed decision about what initiatives to remove, I asked my staff three simple questions (see Image 8.1):

1. What are you hoping to accomplish?

2. What barriers stand in your way?

3. How can I support you?

I was surprised to learn that it wasn't the legislation that was overwhelming. It was the number of meetings about the legislation and the paperwork that went with the meetings.

I placed a piece of butcher paper in the staff lounge and asked, "If we don't want meetings, what do we want?" Perhaps it was the anonymity. Perhaps it was the fact that teachers could answer when they had an idea as opposed to being forced into brainstorming. Whatever the reason, the responses poured in.

We decided to establish a Google Classroom to share essential information and updates in a centralized location. This way, team members could access it at their convenience, reducing the need for meetings to disseminate the details. Teachers were thankful for the compilation of resources, and teams held one another accountable. It was a win-win.

One of the most important gifts principals can give their teachers is time. Time, unfortunately, is limited, so we need to find ways to manage the time we have. One way is to minimize distractions by removing unnecessary tasks teachers must accomplish. This might include unnecessary PD, discipline issues, and mandates.

While some of these categories are outside of our sphere of control, we do get to control the way in which we present them to our staff. Sometimes minimizing distractions means letting go of the tasks we wanted to do as administrators to take care of the action items we collectively decided to do as a team. Focus on the following:

- Have your team's backs.
- Create a positive atmosphere, even in the midst of challenges.
- Reassess and refine what you ask your teachers to do.
- Filter out as many distractions as you can.

All this enables your teachers and staff to do what they are meant to do and honor their why.

HACK 9

EMPHASIZE TRUST OVER TRANSFORMATION

Establish Relational Trust Before Making Changes

Trust is the glue of life. It's the most essential ingredient in effective communication. It's the foundational principle that holds all relationships.
—STEPHEN COVEY, AUTHOR, EDUCATOR, AND BUSINESSMAN

THE PROBLEM: WE WANT CHANGE NOW

EDUCATORS WANT CHANGE right away. This comes from a wonderful place, as we desire what is best for our students. However, effective change takes time. Even more importantly, it takes trust. Trust is the first building block when it comes to psychological safety. Too often, principals try to make change without first building trust. Unfortunately, in the absence of trust, we won't get far.

A lack of trust comes from a leader's actions or inactions. Many educators have had bad experiences with leadership, making them predisposed to mistrust. Perhaps this is the result of mismanagement, micromanagement, or a strong belief in positional power dynamics.

Being inconsistent, failing to own mistakes, lacking vulnerability, and avoiding connection are all trust-breakers. While we may not exhibit these behaviors intentionally, we also aren't working to improve them with intentionality. And, we *won't* build trust without trying.

Still, this doesn't happen overnight, which frustrates leaders who are ready for change (I am speaking from experience). This impatience often leads to us making fatal flaws such as sharing unclear communication and not knowing our team or their roles. If we don't have trust, we won't have a team. Without a team, we won't have a culture. Without a culture, we fail to move forward for kids. It truly is key to our success as an organization.

THE HACK: EMPHASIZE TRUST OVER TRANSFORMATION

Most teachers are okay with change as long as they trust that it's meaningful. This takes time, and because of its fragile nature, it can ebb and flow. In the strongest organizations, trust is always present, and all stakeholders feel it to some degree.

Trust is essential for a healthy workplace culture, helping people work better with one another and boosting productivity. While we know trust is crucial, we often don't know how to build it intentionally. If you want to build a cohesive school team, you must make trust the foundation of everything you do.

Luckily, we build trust in informal and formal ways. Our daily actions and interactions are equally as crucial as intentional trust-building exercises. The way we carry ourselves as leaders serves as a model for how we want our staff to act. Our actions must be consistent and continuously communicate belonging cues to our staff. This means treating people well, listening, and being aware of our words and actions. In addition, we need to be mindful of what our faces and bodies are telling others. Many times, this is more important than our words. We need to informally check in with our staff and open our doors to every person, no matter their role.

We can also build trust between staff members and encourage them to become a team. Creating experiences for staff to interact with each other is an integral part of building trust. The more interactions we have, the better. Foundationally, trust is about being vulnerable with one another and motivated to continue experiencing success together.

WHAT YOU CAN DO TOMORROW

As mentioned, building trust takes time, and you must actively and intentionally work on it throughout the days, weeks, months, and years. While many trust-building strategies are ongoing, you can start tomorrow and take steps to build up that foundation. Remember, never underestimate the power of small actions and moments.

- **Tell the truth.** While being honest seems like an obvious first step in building trust, we often veer away from it for the sake of comfort. Even the simplest fib can kill your credibility. Transparency is an act of kindness, even when it's awkward. Sometimes it's hard to be honest in the moment when we get hung up on what people want to hear.

However, being transparent is more important than being nice. Of course, approach the truth with sensitivity to people's feelings but tell people what they need to know, even when it's uncomfortable. If you build a reputation as someone who is dishonest, you break trust and rarely get it back.

- **Commit to listening.** Being an active listener is so much more important than being someone who has all the answers. Pay attention to how much you speak and how much you listen. You'll likely find an imbalance. We tend to talk *at* our staff rather than *with* them. This can lead to an imbalance of trust and often takes away from the psychological safety of our team. Every person desires to be heard. Active listening communicates to other people that they are safe, they are valued, and they belong.

  Sending feedback signals is a way to show others you are interested in what they have to say. These include:

  - ▸ body language and facial expressions
  - ▸ reflection through paraphrasing to clarify information
  - ▸ asking questions
  - ▸ withholding judgment when someone says something you disagree with

- **Treat people well and show genuine interest.** Show people that you care about them outside of what they do professionally. Ask questions and remember personal details (take notes later if you need to). Greeting people by name and engaging them in conversations about their lives and interests shows you authentically care about them. We all know it's much more difficult to trust someone who seems self-serving and uninterested.

A BLUEPRINT FOR FULL IMPLEMENTATION

Step 1: Lead with trust.

Lead with trust, and trust will follow. More than anything, teachers don't want to be micromanaged. They want others to see and treat them as professionals and give them autonomy to make decisions that best support their students and classrooms. When we extend trust to the people we serve, we invite reciprocity toward ourselves and the greater community. Is this a risk? Absolutely. However, it's a risk worth taking.

When people feel trusted, not only are they more likely to trust you in return, but they also will likely work harder and accomplish more. Trusting others allows you the opportunity to delegate and, ultimately, multiply leadership, which only serves to strengthen the school environment. For example, you may recognize teachers doing a good job and ask them to take on leadership roles. You share why you trusted them, highlighting the strengths and the reasons you know they will be successful. As a result, these teachers work to live up to your expectations. Your staff notices that you have trusted others with leadership and begins to emulate the positive behaviors. This impacts and strengthens the entire school environment.

A caveat: In extending trust, we must also identify the limitations. For example, it may be okay for teachers or staff to walk into school when the students do. However, students obviously need supervision. You don't need to collect lesson plans; however, you do need teachers to be able to articulate what they want students to know and do. Be transparent about your limitations regarding school happenings, and stick to them.

> **When we extend trust to the people we serve, we invite reciprocity toward ourselves and the greater community.**

Step 2: Let go.

Extending trust isn't just about what you expect. In many instances, it's also about what you are willing to let go. It's about giving people the benefit of the doubt and assuming positive intentions. No matter what, you need to be authentic; teachers and staff know the difference.

Step 3: Take time to connect.

Make time to connect with those you serve. This not only builds trust but also maintains it. While finding the time to connect with everyone can be difficult, it's certainly worth it.

You can stay in touch with your team in formal and informal ways. Being visible in the building during the school day is easy, informal, and effective. Asking teachers how they are doing, inquiring about their lives outside of school, and following up about a special occasion take forethought yet add so much value.

More formally, set aside time to intentionally touch base with your people. During the summer, create a sign-up form to talk with teachers. While not everyone will take you up on the offer, you're providing the opportunity. Use the time to ask them what's going well, what's not working, and what ideas they have for improving the school.

Formal connections can also happen during the school year. Ask teachers to meet with you once a semester during their planning time to connect. You don't need an agenda; just ask how they're doing and let the conversation flow freely. You get bonus points if you arrange coverage for teachers to have these connection meetings outside their planning time. These conversations don't have to be mandated, but tracking who has taken the time to reach out is a good idea. Sending a thank you note after you talk is a nice touch that shows your gratitude for their time.

Step 4: Be intentional.

While this seems obvious, school days are busy, and the small interactions needed to build trust are often lost or forgotten. Intentionally use your actions and words to build and maintain trust. Here are a few ways:

- **Genuinely listen:** Block out noise or distractions to focus on the person doing the talking. Many times, we are listening to respond instead of to understand what the person is saying. This is a tough skill to master, but it's a critical one.

- **Be around:** We tend to trust those who we are more familiar with. The only way for people to become more familiar with you as a leader is to be visible and create multiple interactions with them. Think about how you might create positive interactions without constantly being in their space. For example, before the school day begins is a good time to take a walk around the building and engage in short conversations.

- **Talk straight:** People don't want leaders who are simply nice; they respect people who own their realities. After all, we can't fix what we don't know. Sometimes the kindest gesture is to talk straight, even when the news isn't positive. This doesn't mean you delete your filter; it means you don't avoid truths that your team needs to know for each of you to grow and be successful.

Step 5: Be vulnerable.

We can't possibly know the outcomes of every situation and circumstance, but as leaders, we need to show up and take the risk of events not going as planned. This is vulnerability. It is essential to trust, and it helps those we serve to see us as human. Vulnerability means stepping outside of our comfort zone. First, we need to know ourselves and our comfort zones. Journaling is a highly insightful way to do this. It doesn't have to be time-consuming or fraught with emotion. Find a journal that asks one question or a few questions daily. (Check out *Permission to Pause: A Journal for Teachers* by Dorothy VanderJagt.) Over time, it'll help you get inside your head and better understand your strengths and limitations.

Admitting you don't have all the answers is another way to own your vulnerability. When you express this to your staff, they'll be more likely to admit it to you. People need to see leaders asking for help or seeking answers from other sources. It's okay to be honest if you're having a hard time or feeling anxious. While you should avoid projecting these feelings onto your staff, it's okay to own the feelings. It normalizes how hard this job can be.

Step 6: Say what you do, do what you say.

Consistency leads to predictability, and predictability leads to trust. We've all had leaders with inconsistent actions where we never know what to expect. As a result, our amygdala gets hijacked.

People can't do their best work when scanning the environment for safety. Transparency and consistency help people feel psychologically safe, and when people feel safe, they can learn and grow.

So, how does one stay consistent?

- **Define and communicate your mission:** Commit to your mission wholeheartedly. For example, let's say your mission is to help people believe that everyone should belong without compromising who they are. Every decision you make is grounded in this goal. People will always know what to expect. Then, when you make a decision that they don't like, they will still understand why you made it.

- **Pay attention to your actions:** As you go through your day, pay attention to what you do, what you say, and how you say it. Be sure to compare your words and actions to your mission, and note any discrepancies. Reflect on how or why you behaved differently than your intentions. Part of this is about monitoring your moods and attitudes. Pay attention to what triggers you and choose to do those activities when you don't need to be at your best. For example, if you know that checking your email is a trigger, check it when people are gone at the end of the day.

- **Communicate:** Articulate the reasons behind your actions and decisions so your team understands who you are and what you stand for. Sometimes we get so caught up in the message or the decision that we forget to communicate its rationale. Yet, in many instances, the rationale matters more. Remember that communication is not a monologue but rather a dialogue. Hold regular check-ins with your staff so you, too, can understand their mission and rationale. To gain trust, you also need to extend it.

Transparency and consistency help people feel psychologically safe, and when people feel safe, they can learn and grow.

Step 7: Establish accountability for yourself and one another.

Accountability creates systems that avoid nonexistent or unclear goals, miscommunications, or inconsistent outcomes. Systems work proactively and reactively to provide clear expectations and measurable results.

Note: There's a difference between accountability and micromanagement. Accountability clearly defines roles and responsibilities so your staff are empowered to work within those guidelines, whereas micromanagement defines *how* staff should accomplish their roles and responsibilities. It also encourages them to take more responsibility for what happens within the school. While there's no one way to develop a system of accountability, a few factors are imperative:

- **Establish clear roles:** Your staff need to know precisely what they are responsible for and what they are not with every task within the school, and they need some say in defining those roles and responsibilities. Establish a method to define and communicate these expectations.

- **Monitor progress:** Find consistent ways to measure progress toward goals. Not only is this important to replicate success, but it's also essential to know how you might adjust.

- **Articulate and follow through with consistent, reasonable consequences:** Defining the limits will help you all know what you're trying to accomplish and where you are in terms of progress. However, it is equally essential for staff to understand what might happen if they or the team falls short or doesn't follow through. The fastest way to harm trust is to have inconsistent responses for unmet responsibilities. Communicate what will happen next, then take steps to get there.

- **Celebrate success:** If people are doing the right thing in the right way, point it out and celebrate it. Success is essential to accountability, since it builds trust and buy-in.

OVERCOMING PUSHBACK

The scariest part of trust is that we must often first extend it to receive it. Many leaders have a hard time giving trust because of negative past experiences. We hold people accountable for the mistakes others have made and, therefore, tend to err on the side of over-direction and micromanagement. We either believe we *are* extending trust or that people don't deserve trust. The reality is that everyone deserves trust until they don't, and then it should come down to personal conversations and not generic email messages to everyone. Building trust is a continuous process, and it's vital to your team's success. Still, many will argue against it.

I already do that. Many people feel that they are already extending trust; therefore, they don't have to continue to work on it with intentionality. But trust isn't a one-and-done concept. You need to continuously build trust because you are certainly going to lose some. Make sure people are willing to pick up the pieces and start again. This extends past your teachers to all the people within your organization. Trust isn't a task on a checklist; it should be the basis for everything you do and plan to do.

People won't do the work. Many people worry that if they extend trust without step-by-step instructions, people won't fulfill their responsibilities. However, more than anything, teachers do not want to be micromanaged. They want others to see them as professionals with the autonomy to make the best decisions regarding their students and meeting their needs. Teachers are professionals, and everyone should treat them as such. Teachers go above and beyond when they are empowered by trust. This is not to say that you don't define the nonnegotiables; however, allowing freedoms within these limits gives teachers the autonomy they want and need.

I've been burned before. It's true. We've all been burned by giving trust to people who either abused it or didn't deserve it in the first place. Certainly, there will be people who fall short of expectations, but it means far more to everyone if those conversations happen individually and you don't hold the entire organization responsible for the failure of one. Teachers want to do right by kids. They want to do right by their teammates. They want to do right by the school. Sometimes, however, a failed understanding of organizational vision and goals can cause a breakdown in trust. Ensure that everyone knows the shared mission and vision and that the direction is well-established.

In addition, extending trust doesn't mean you don't have expectations and accountability structures. It simply means you have clearly defined limits and extend freedom within them. Yes, you may get burned. Yes, you may get burned again. However, the benefits of developing trust far outweigh the costs of lacking trust.

THE HACK IN ACTION

Each action we take has the potential to build trust or destroy it. One of the fastest ways to destroy trust is through a lack of consistency. No one likes having hard conversations, but if trust is present, there are no hard conversations, only conversations.

If you have been a teacher, you know what spring feels like. There is a lot of stress around which educators will be moving grade levels, classrooms, or teams. With that stress comes conversations, gossip, and anxiety. As a principal, I dislike this environment, yet I've learned that although we can't completely alleviate it, some circumstances give us no choice but to make changes.

Each year, teachers fill out a grade-level preference survey. They can inform me of their first, second, and third choices regarding grade levels. It's rare for someone to request a change of grade. Most of the time, they request to stay where they are with the same teammates. In my first year as principal, those were the responses of all the teachers. In my second year, teachers still chose their grade levels, but their comments changed. Most of the comments said something to the effect of "I trust you, and I will go wherever you think is best." It was a noticeable shift ... and it caused me to stop and reflect in gratitude.

I had a conversation with one of the teachers about why they felt more flexibility, and she said, "You always put the kids first. If you move me, I know it is because of the kids." The consistency of my actions and words mattered in this situation. It's comforting to know what to expect from someone. You never have to ask why because you already know the answer. That's what happened in my case. Teachers learned that my actions would match my why, and my why was the same as theirs—our students.

Teachers need their principals' trust, which creates a positive work environment, fosters collaboration, and supports professional growth. Additionally, trust enables teachers to take risks and be innovative in their teaching practices, leading to improved student outcomes.

Teachers often feel that others don't see them as professionals or experts, yet this is what they want more than anything. They want the freedom to do what is best for their students and the trust to do so in a way that might be different from what we, as leaders, would do. Micromanagement is the enemy of freedom. It's not that teachers don't want boundaries; they do. However, they want some say and choice in those boundaries and freedom within the limits.

While this might work differently than we imagine in our minds as administrators, we need to let go of what we think is best to give room for teachers to try, fail, pick up the pieces, and try again.

HACK 10

BUILD BELONGING
Create Conditions for Authenticity without Compromise

I belong to the people I love, and they belong to me—
they, and the love and loyalty I give them, form my
identity far more than any word or group ever could.
—VERONICA ROTH, AUTHOR

THE PROBLEM: PEOPLE CAN'T BE THEIR AUTHENTIC SELVES

BELONGING IS A basic human need and is more than simply being part of a group. It's about acceptance, validation, affirmation, and genuine connection. One problem with belonging is that we often mistake it for diversity or inclusion. These are pertinent to organizations but are, in many ways, one-way extensions, whereas belonging is reciprocal. I've often said that diversity is about numbers: for example, the number of people from different backgrounds and cultures we are fortunate to attract. In that sense, inclusion is about what you do with those numbers. Belonging is

147

about turning those numbers into humans without expecting them to change any part of their identity to fit in.

Certainly, we still must focus on building a diverse staff through policy changes, recruitment efforts, and retention efforts and provide professional learning that builds competencies. But we need to do this *and* hold ourselves accountable for ensuring that every person in our building feels safe and connected and both trusts and feels trusted within our community. It's hard work, but it's the right work.

As leaders, creating a culture of belonging is a challenge because we have constant distractions such as discipline, facility issues, and sub shortages. While these distractions are certainly part of the work, they make it a challenge to consistently focus on the people. Many times, the work of establishing belonging happens behind the scenes. It's in the text messages, the check-ins, and the intentional listening, but most of all, it's in truly seeing people … seeing each person, not just all people.

Another challenge is that we can't "see" true belonging; we "feel" it. This makes it hard to quantify. To accurately measure it, you must rely on people to be open and honest. This doesn't happen often because we don't take the time or we don't have the trust of our team (see Hack 9 for help with this). Unfortunately, many people have had past experiences of being *othered*, which means they've been treated badly or made to feel as though they don't belong.

THE HACK: BUILD BELONGING

To be honest, we can't hack belonging. Still, it's imperative to create a feeling of belonging as part of our people-centered leadership; without belonging, it's difficult for people to do their best work. It's hard to get them invested in the work if they don't feel like contributing members. There is no doubt that prioritizing inclusion and belonging leads to happiness and satisfaction for your teachers, staff, and entire community.

Building belonging is a long-term and daily commitment to the people within your organization. However, you can certainly take some small, high-leverage steps to help people feel seen, valued, connected, and appreciated.

Why is belonging essential within an organization? It has many ties to job satisfaction and engagement. But even more critical is its impact on each individual. Education often comes with an underrepresentation of diverse staff. While recruitment efforts have increased, retention efforts are inconsistent. We must create a culture where every member of your team feels like they belong.

> **You cannot expect those who are oppressed or marginalized to carry the load for those who don't understand firsthand what it means to be underserved.**

Building this culture begins with a collective understanding of who you are as an organization, starting with a vision or mission that all members create together. While you may not do this every year, you'll want to at least revisit it every year to ensure your mission and vision still represent the people inside the walls and the work you are trying to do together. While collective vision is important, it is a delicate dance, as you also need space for individuals to be who they are without compromise. This means they can be comfortable as their authentic selves.

Belonging looks different to every individual. What makes one person feel they belong might look different from another, depending on whether they are from an underrepresented group within the organization, what cultural or linguistic population they identify with, and various other personal traits. To build belonging, we can't think of people as a single, unified, or indivisible entity. Individuals are simply that ... unique individuals.

The responsibility for developing a strong and accepting community doesn't only fall to the principal or building leader. All people across the organization must multiply it. As leaders, we can create enthusiasm for learning about our colleagues and understanding what each one needs to feel they belong. Opportunities come through providing time for social interactions and collaborations and creating the physical space within the building for both.

Consider how you form teams or committees and build bridges between leadership, classroom teachers, specialists, and support staff. And, yes, I know many people hate icebreakers and get-to-know-you activities. So, being intentional and thoughtful in these interactions and collaborations will take away some of the negativity that can come with such activities.

Yet, how do you measure belonging? This is no small feat, particularly when positional power exists and trust (again) is vital. You can empower every individual on your team and create the circumstances where people can be their authentic selves. Ask questions about belonging, even if you don't like the answers. And then use that data to establish a better environment within your school and within yourself.

WHAT YOU CAN DO TOMORROW

Although creating a culture of belonging is a long-term commitment, you can find ways to kickstart it. Remember that trust is the foundation of belonging—allowing individuals to show up, be their true selves, and connect with others. So, start creating an authentic culture tomorrow and keep building on it every day.

- **Check the pulse.** Right now, you can do a quick check about how people feel regarding their belonging. This doesn't have to be overwhelming or time-consuming; simply asking your staff these two questions yields information:

  1. Do you feel like this is the school for you?
  2. Do you feel like you can be your true self here?

  Their answers won't necessarily give you information about how to make people feel affirmed and included, but they will give you a general idea about where your staff stands as a whole. This doesn't have to be formal. A Google Form is quick and convenient, and it offers general information. Image 10.1 shows a survey we sometimes share with younger students.

If you want communication between you and your staff, hope alone doesn't cut it.

Belonging Survey

Name_____

Grade   K   1   2   3   4   5

1. I feel like this is the right school for me.

Yes   No

2. I can be my true self at this school.

Yes   No

3. If I have a problem at this school, there's an adult or teacher I can talk to.

Yes   No

Image 10.1

- **Develop your equity lens.** You can't learn everything you need to know about diversity, equity, and inclusion tomorrow, but what you can do is either begin or continue to develop your equity lens. If you want to build a culture of belonging, it's imperative to know and understand both the historical and current implications of bias and racism. Reading books and articles, watching documentaries, and familiarizing yourself with cultures different from yours are essential to knowing and supporting your staff.

An equity lens will help you to be more deliberate with inclusion and belonging so you will understand what to consider when making decisions. Look at your overall organization and find the gaps. Recognize that leaders are from different places and cultures, so your views on equity may look different than theirs.

Note: You cannot expect those who are oppressed or marginalized to carry the load for those who don't understand firsthand what it means to be underserved. One has to develop their own knowledge and understanding. This won't happen tomorrow, but starting now is imperative.

- **Put your cell phone down.** Most everyone is distracted. We've all experienced having a conversation with someone and they pick up their cell phone or check their smartwatch. It makes us feel as though we are interrupting or bothering them. As a result, the connection is broken. As administrators, we are often overly connected to our devices, constantly checking our phones or emails. While the intent is to ensure we aren't needed somewhere, the impact is that we are breaking a connection with people in our presence. Without connection, we won't have trust. Without trust, we won't have belonging. Be mindful of distractions when you are building connections. Figure out ways to build connections, not break them. Be present in the now.

- **Schedule communication.** Make time for your teachers to connect with you and with one another. If you want communication between you and your staff, hope alone doesn't cut it. Prioritize communication by scheduling time on your calendar. While the conversations won't all happen tomorrow, you can begin planning for them. When do you want these conversations to take place? How often? How do you ensure they don't create more work or stress for your teachers?

A BLUEPRINT FOR FULL IMPLEMENTATION

Step 1: Invest in identity work.

If we want to keep people from compromising who they are, they first need to *know* who they are. Identity work is key so everyone understands the individual role they play within a school. Exploring identity allows us to see ourselves and one another. It allows us to own our strengths and challenges to grow ourselves and others.

Understanding our identity also creates a sense of belonging and a desire to help others feel this same sense of community. Leaders can provide intentional opportunities for their staff to reflect on who they are and how to respect others—knowing, of course, that identity is not static.

Identity webs are an effective way to start and are a great visual for helping others understand who we are. They begin with your name in a circle and then contain various parts of your identity in circles that extend out. These include the qualities, beliefs, and traits that make you who you are. While not everyone will feel comfortable sharing every aspect of their identities, the team can establish those aspects that impact how they work with one another.

At the beginning of each year, I ask individuals to develop webs to share with their teams. While they can include any aspect of their personal culture they choose, I ask them to include these four:

▶ What helps me thrive?

▶ What shuts me down?

▶ What do I always do?

▶ What do I appreciate from others?

Journaling is another way to explore identity. You can encourage your staff to keep a journal and record thoughts, feelings, and experiences related to their identity. They can use the journal throughout the year as a space for self-reflection, introspection, and exploring different aspects of who they are.

Self-reflection exercises—such as asking people to answer thought-provoking questions about their values, beliefs, strengths, weaknesses, and life goals—are another way to do identity work. Engaging in conversations regarding these exercises helps staff understand the identities of each other.

We all have strengths and challenges. Knowing what to expect from others and how to respond to one another will help to build a connection. We can explore our identities in many ways; the important part is that we do it.

Step 2: Share the vision.

The world can be polarizing. As educators, we constantly defend our work, practices, and beliefs. This is partly because, as a society, people tend to focus on what they are against. Instead, we need to focus on what we are for. One way to do this is through a shared vision, compiling the goals and dreams of what we hope to accomplish together. Define the following as a group:

- Who do we want to be?
- What do we hope to accomplish?
- How will we know we've accomplished it?
- What will we do if we fall short of our vision?
- What will we do when we are successful?

Asking individuals to answer these questions and then to discuss, compare, and compile the goals is a terrific way to start a school year, build buy-in, and create a community based on trust.

Step 3: Encourage employee resource groups.

These groups are made up of people who have a commonality within their identities. Typically, the characteristic that ties these individuals together places them in an underserved or underrepresented group. Perhaps being underrepresented *is* the commonality. Employee resource groups help people in diverse populations feel belonging, offering support for those facing the same challenges within a school.

As a principal, you likely won't be the one establishing these groups, but you can encourage them. In addition, providing opportunities for the groups to give feedback and input to create a safer space for all will multiply the feeling of belonging. While many schools lack diverse staff, this might be an effort that extends to the district as a whole. Successful employee resource groups are not easy, but many good resources exist regarding how to establish them and help them grow. Search online and you will find options for resources. Principals need to do what they can to build belonging. Employee resource groups are one way to support that mission.

> **Remember that everyone is at a different place regarding equity and belonging work, so make room for differentiation and choice.**

Step 4: Make belonging the rule and not the exception.

Too often in the work of diversity, equity, and inclusion, we expect those experiencing underrepresentation and -isms to teach everyone else in the group about diversity, equity, and inclusion. Yet, it's exhausting to those already doing the heavy lifting. Create an expectation that every staff member continues to grow regarding your team's equity and belonging efforts. This doesn't just matter to teachers but to the entire school community.

And—just as importantly—make time and space for this work. Equity hubs, book studies, and focus groups are ways to learn and grow together. If you want to build belonging, you need to work to understand the different perspectives of others. This is a nonnegotiable.

Remember that everyone is at a different place regarding equity and belonging work, so make room for differentiation and choice. It's not important where you start; it's only important that you continuously move forward. The following strategies build consistent learning:

- **Equity hubs:** This can look different depending on your school and the staff's needs. Perhaps it's a Google Classroom, blog, or website. No matter what you decide, this is a place to house resources for building equity and belonging for everyone in your building. This saves your teachers time and allows you to select resources that will help them grow and learn. All staff members can contribute to this hub. It's not enough just to provide this resource, however. You must provide the time to use it, such as building exploration time into your PD plans.

- **Book studies:** These are an excellent way to discuss belonging. You can offer a choice of titles, or teachers can choose a book to read around the general theme of belonging. This allows teachers the opportunity to further their growth and learning. Again, provide the time to do this work.

- **Belonging challenge:** Bring resources together, such as podcasts, books, articles, blogs, movies, and TV shows. Throughout a period of time (thirty days, a semester, the year), ask teachers to engage in X number of activities. Provide time along the way for check-in meetings, either with a set group or flexible groups. Again, you have to prioritize this work. End the year with a celebration of growth. Teachers could use an "I used to think ... but now I think ..." structure.

You can deploy so many ways of prioritizing this work. Just make sure it is the rule and not the exception. We all value what we give time to.

Step 5: Measure your growth.

Use the growth measurement defined in your shared mission to assess the atmosphere of belonging in your school ... for staff as well as students. You and your team need to know that your efforts are working. If they aren't, you need to understand why. This can be as simple or as complex as you wish. The most important aspect of collecting data is to ensure that it is representative of the entire staff and school. While collecting names on surveys can be a deterrent, knowing who doesn't feel comfortable providing their name is also essential. That, in itself, is data. Collecting email addresses allows you to have the follow-up conversations necessary to build context. Still, this won't happen without trust. Use the data to move your school forward. Here's a quick survey I use:

ADULT BELONGING SURVEY

1. What do you love about our school?

2. What would you change about our school?

3. How do you like to be recognized?

4. What keeps you working here?

5. What would make your job better?

6. What talents do you have that you wish were being used?

OVERCOMING PUSHBACK

Intentional work on belonging can feel like *one more thing* when everyone in education is already doing so much. However, remember that people feeling like they belong *is* the *thing*. Equity should be seen and felt in every aspect of the school, and a sense of belonging should always be the focus for every student, teacher, and staff member. Of course, there is the concern that people won't do the work or be honest. Regardless, you owe it to the people in your building to do this work and do it well. Pushback is always present, particularly in a polarizing world. Still, you can find ways to address that pushback.

Not everyone believes in this work. If they don't believe in this work, perhaps it's time to point them in another direction. Schools are full of diverse human beings. You owe it to your staff and students to work together and create safe spaces. Establish a culture where you are united in what you're fighting for as opposed to separated by what you're against. It's hard to argue with a desire to make the school a place where everyone can be authentic without compromising. Focus on humanizing your people, not on the political views and oppositions that get in the way.

We don't have enough time. If you make time for only one thing, it should be the psychological safety of each person in your building. Without psychological safety, our brains continue to scan the world for threats. When our brains are focused on protection, they can't form social bonds and they can't learn. Take time to ensure that each member of your staff has what they need to feel that they can be themselves without having to change to fit in. Knowing and understanding who is in your organization and how you can make them feel they are a part of your community isn't just crucial for teachers and students; it's essential for the entire organization.

Teachers won't be honest with their feelings. Create the circumstances for teachers to be open and honest with their emotions. This involves trust. Trying to do this work without first building trust will be fruitless. Work hard to cultivate relationships and understanding so people know you are here for them. Be honest. It's okay if you haven't gotten very far in creating a strong sense of belonging in your building, but it's not okay *not* to move forward. It takes intentional work and honesty … that is the most important job of a leader.

THE HACK IN ACTION

by Marie Thomas, educator

I have been incredibly lucky to work for an awesome administrator who showed gratitude, prioritized my well-being, built relational trust and belonging, and provided me with specific and meaningful feedback. Although I am diligent in my work, I am also a highly anxious person. While I do not mind going the extra mile in any endeavor I take on, it makes me anxious and uncomfortable when others call me out publicly for anything, either positively or negatively. I do not want public kudos. I do not want anyone to call on me. I do not want anyone to single me out.

Over several years, I was fortunate to work for the same administrator, who seemed to know this about me. He never drew attention to me in public situations. However, he always made sure to let me know that he appreciated my efforts via email or a private comment while passing in the hall. I would often hear through the grapevine that he had made positive comments about my work ethic or my rapport with the kids.

In addition to this, my principal was incredibly easy to talk to and would often shoulder an additional burden that he knew I could not handle. This included smoothing things over when I made little mistakes or playing things off as nothing at all when I knew in my heart that they were bigger than he made them out to be.

He simply let me be.

I am sure he knew that my overthinking would be more than enough of a correction and that he didn't need to say anything at all. This type of acceptance and understanding gave me increased confidence as a teacher in addition to creating room for me to improve myself, either through courses or experience. He was always pushing me to do better and be better. He really did bring out the best in me.

This administrator was so in tune with his staff that he knew when things were bothering people just by looking at them. I distinctly recall passing him in the hall one day, and just a few minutes later, I received an email that said, "My door's open." This was typical of him, and I appreciated it.

I was able to be myself without having to sugarcoat what I wanted to say. I could be honest, and he always had something positive to say or a different perspective or lens for me to view the situation through. I appreciated this so much. This sort of relational trust also led me to feel like I truly belonged at this school; it truly felt like home. Any time I needed to speak with him, he shut off his phone, turned his computer screen away, and focused his attention on me as though I were the only person he had to deal with that day. I never had to compete for his time.

This made me happy to work for this principal. I would have volunteered for any activity, club, sport, event … you name it! Even if it were out of my wheelhouse, I would figure out a way to make it work. When you have an exceptional leader like this one, you don't mind reciprocating in an attempt to make things great for the school and for the kids. I often joked that I would work for him half-price.

I have since changed schools (not by choice), but he continues to mentor me and provide me with meaningful feedback to the best of his ability. He doesn't need to do this, but I feel that he has a genuine investment in the kids, in the school, and in his people. He was the best administrator I have ever worked for, without a doubt!

Belonging is the outcome we hope for regarding diversity and inclusion. Helping people feel safe to be their authentic selves is an important part of being a leader who creates a thriving culture of learning. Without creating opportunities for people to learn about themselves and the identities of others, it will be hard, if not impossible, to build a strong community.

While this work can feel uncomfortable and time-consuming, it's necessary. We want people to dig deep into the differences that make our schools exceptional. We need to see race and ethnicity and gender. If we don't see them, we won't be able to understand and address the -isms that impact belonging. It's a commitment to our staff, our students, and our community.

DEVELOP HUMANS OVER HEROES
End the Superhero Narrative

The "teacher as superhero" narrative is problematic because it places unrealistic expectations on teachers and implies that their value is measured by their ability to work miracles in the classroom.
—DR. KEVIN KUMASHIRO, EDUCATION SCHOLAR AND AUTHOR

THE PROBLEM: TEACHERS ARE EXPECTED TO DO IT ALL

PEOPLE FREQUENTLY USE expressions like "magicians" or "superheroes" when praising teachers. While this narrative is not inherently harmful, it can become detrimental when used to undermine realistic expectations and the significance of teachers and the education system.

Teachers often face immense pressure with the expectation that they possess the ability to solve complex societal problems effortlessly. This expectation unfairly burdens teachers, leading to heightened stress levels and unrealistic demands. Teachers are increasingly pushed into situations where they are expected to singlehandedly address deep-rooted issues such as poverty, educational inequities, bullying, and unsafe social media practices.

Teachers are neither magicians nor superheroes (see Hack 1). They are hard workers who put hours and hours into what they do. And without support from administrators, colleagues, and society, teachers have a difficult time succeeding. In fact, when teachers are called heroes, it emphasizes the lack of importance placed on education and the role teachers play.

By the way, superheroes don't use the restroom, and we rarely see them sleep. How often has Spiderman's boss come around to ensure he has what he needs to serve the community?

Education is a collective responsibility. When we place educators on a pedestal as superheroes, it shifts the responsibility away from collaborative efforts and places the bulk of the responsibility on teachers. Not only does this take away from the systemic issues that we need to address, such as inequities and mental health crises, but it also diminishes the collaborative efforts required from all stakeholders to enhance the education system. Educators need society to support them rather than rely on them individually. We, as leaders, need to work intentionally to make this happen.

Teachers are human beings. They need support, praise, and resources in order to be successful. While the superhero narrative is used as a compliment for how wonderful teachers are and how much they accomplish, it also (likely unintentionally) diminishes the dedication, hard work, and long hours teachers spend trying to ensure all students learn at high levels in a place where they feel safe and feel they belong.

THE HACK: DEVELOP HUMANS OVER HEROES

It's important for administrators to treat teachers as humans and not heroes by ensuring that the targets and expectations they set are realistic. This motivates teachers and provides a clear direction for their work. The belief that goals are attainable helps teachers feel a sense of accomplishment and satisfaction when they achieve them. This is incredibly important in today's world, when it feels like targets are constantly moving and changing.

In addition, realistic expectations create a sense of purpose and calm by eliminating the overwhelming and stressed-out feelings that can come from unrealistic administrators. It can be damaging to hold on to where students should be when our world is changing. Allowing teachers the flexibility to focus on what is true today rather than yesterday creates an environment where they can experience success rather than failure.

In addition, setting realistic targets also enables teachers to enhance their overall performance. When teachers clearly understand the expectations placed upon them and believe those goals are achievable, they can focus their efforts and leverage their skills and expertise to their fullest potential.

Advocating for realistic targets does not imply lowering the standards or compromising on the pursuit of excellence. The aim remains to ensure the success of every student. However, it may necessitate a shift in the definition of standards. While academic outcomes held significant importance in the past, social-emotional development has emerged as a more relevant focus today.

By acknowledging social-emotional targets alongside academic goals, we can foster a more comprehensive approach to education. This recognizes the holistic needs of students, promoting their emotional well-being, interpersonal skills, and resilience alongside their academic growth. In doing so, we create a more balanced and realistic educational environment.

When we focus on developing humans instead of heroes, we also motivate teachers to improve. Achievable goals and measurable targets help them focus on specific improvements. Thus, teachers continue to grow and achieve new targets through ongoing professional development. This, in turn, creates better student outcomes. When teachers focus on what they can and should realistically achieve in the classroom, they provide a high-quality education to their students and help them reach their full potential.

> *While academic outcomes held significant importance in the past, social-emotional development has emerged as a more relevant focus today.*

Another reason why administrators should see teachers as humans and not heroes is that it fosters a more supportive and collaborative school culture. When teachers feel that administrators value them as individuals, they are more likely to share their ideas, collaborate with their colleagues, and engage in ongoing professional development. This leads to more significant innovation and creativity in the classroom and a more supportive and collaborative school environment. Additionally, when teachers feel they are part of a team rather than just individuals solving tough issues, they are more likely to seek help and support when needed, leading to better outcomes for both them and their students.

WHAT YOU CAN DO TOMORROW

The teacher as superhero narrative is problematic because it places unrealistic expectations on teachers, which can lead to burnout—or worse, teachers leaving the profession. Reversing this mentality will take time. It's not that teachers aren't amazing, but to call them heroes certainly diminishes all they do to ensure they are what students need. Happily, you can begin tomorrow to ensure that the community and your teachers themselves know their hard work is seen, felt, and appreciated.

- **Use alternative language.** While meant as a compliment, calling teachers superheroes or magicians removes the focus from their skills, expertise, and dedication. The intent is good; the impact can be harmful. Different words to describe teachers can recognize their hard work and dedication without reducing them to mythical or superhuman figures. Instead of focusing on language like "superheroes" or "rock stars," use more concrete and specific language to acknowledge their work and accomplishments. For example, terms like "mentor," "guide," "expert," or "leader" are more effective in recognizing the value and impact teachers have on their students. Additionally, emphasizing the importance of empathy, patience, and compassion in teaching creates a culture of respect and appreciation for the human qualities that teachers bring to their work. Using language that reflects the true nature of education as a skilled and dedicated profession honors and celebrates the hard work and commitment of teachers while also creating a more accurate and realistic view of their role in education.

- **Focus on the system, not the individual.** When we focus on the teacher as the sole reason that education succeeds, we inadvertently blame them as the sole reason when it fails. Instead, highlight the importance of funding, policy, and systemic change. Redirect the focus from the individual to the team or the system. This emphasizes the collective whole, which is essential because educational success depends on a solid strategy that supports teachers, students, and families. No one person can make this happen. Also, no one person can make it fail.

- **Celebrate all educators.** We've all made the mistake of talking about teachers, even though we mean everyone on our team. Recognizing the importance of all roles and the need for collaboration and teamwork can take the pressure off teachers while still acknowledging their value.

A BLUEPRINT FOR FULL IMPLEMENTATION

Principals can set realistic expectations for teachers and staff by following these steps.

Step 1: Build relationships.

While building relationships and trust are stressed throughout this book (especially Hacks 9 and 10), they are vital for this Hack.

When you take the time to understand the needs of your teachers as well as their strengths and weaknesses, you set better, more realistic expectations together.

So, how do you do this?

- **Communicate regularly:** Check in with teachers often and make yourself available in the hallways to answer questions and provide support.

- **Listen without judgment:** Pay attention to their strengths, weaknesses, ideas, and concerns. Work with teachers to solve problems.

- **Support your teachers:** This is a key to success, particularly when it comes to teachers who tend to be people-pleasers. Make yourself available to solve challenges and provide guidance.

- **Show appreciation:** People who feel appreciated are more willing to work harder. Showing appreciation for the hard work that goes on behind the scenes creates an environment where teachers and staff feel valued and motivated.

- **Model the behavior:** You set the tone for the school when you model the behavior you hope to see from your teachers. Behaving in a positive, supportive manner models what you hope to multiply.

> **When you take the time to understand the needs of your teachers as well as their strengths and weaknesses, you set better, more realistic expectations together.**

Step 2: Set goals.

Setting collaborative goals with teachers is an integral part of building realistic expectations. This ensures that principals and teachers work toward common targets and that efforts are aligned with realistic school priorities. Start big. Identify school-wide goals to set an overall direction and purpose. Involving teachers in this process, particularly regarding school-wide objectives, ensures they are achievable and relevant to teachers' needs. From there, you can work collaboratively to set specific realistic goals based on today's realities.

When principals and teachers work collaboratively, they can ensure goals are specific and measurable so they can be tracked and evaluated. Base goals on your staff's strengths and align them with their professional development plans. This not only gives teachers direction regarding *what* to accomplish but also helps them figure out *how*. Then, identifying resources teachers might need helps everyone stay realistic.

Also, for goals to stay realistic, regularly review and evaluate teacher progress and adjust as needed, with flexibility for teachers to stop and change direction. This ensures the goals remain achievable and relevant.

Step 3: Be transparent and specific.

Be transparent and specific regarding goals and expected outcomes. This avoids misunderstandings and allows staff and students to document their efforts on targeted goals. Transparent targets build accountability, as everyone knows what they are working toward and what metric they will use. This encourages everyone to prioritize their efforts and allocate resources effectively.

To be successful, build systems for the development and delivery of expectations. These steps might include the following:

- **Define intended outcomes:** Work with your team to define clear outcomes.

- **Communicate realistic targets:** Clearly and effectively use various communication methods, including staff meetings, newsletters, and conversations.

- **Explain why:** When people know why they are doing something, it encourages buy-in and motivation.

- **Delegate responsibilities:** People need roles and responsibilities that are clearly defined and understood.

- **Measure progress:** Showing how people are growing toward goals is an excellent way to keep staff motivated and engaged.

- **Celebrate successes:** Celebrating successes, whether big or small, keeps staff engaged and builds positivity.

Step 4: Prioritize work-life balance.

For principals to help teachers prioritize work-life balance, they need to model it. When teachers see a principal who has a healthy balance between work and their personal life, it creates a positive school culture. This also means that expectations must be realistic. It helps to ensure we don't overburden our teachers with work and that we give them enough time to complete tasks within the school day.

Providing resources isn't enough. Create a culture where self-care is the rule and not the exception. Figure out how to promote and provide access to exercise, nutrition, sleep, and healthy activities outside of work. Image 11.1 is a visual you can share with your team to encourage them to think about their personal goals.

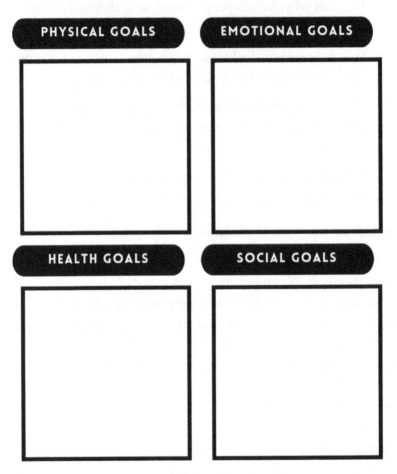

Image 11.1

None of this matters if support is absent. Foster a supportive work environment with open communication, opportunities for collaboration, and recognition of the contributions and achievements of teachers. Professional learning is also part of this support so that staff continue to grow their knowledge and skills.

Step 5: Provide the resources.

In addition to realistic expectations, support and resources are essential and extend far past the curriculum. Principals and districts can and should provide resources to support mental health and well-being, including professional learning, counseling, and mindfulness programs (see Hack 5: Prioritize Well-Being, for more info).

To ensure teachers can do their best work, we, as principals, need to provide them with the right resources. Above all else, communicate regularly to understand teachers' needs and to provide ongoing support. Make yourself available to listen to concerns, feedback, and suggestions, and follow up.

Beyond listening, you can put physical resources into the hands of your teachers. These include professional magazines, books, videos, and online tools. Never underestimate the value of a classroom stocked with modern school supplies.

Other critical resources include collaboration and team-building. Create and maintain opportunities for teachers to work together. Consider shared planning, vertical teaming, mentoring, and executing a think tank.

One example of a think tank came from my school, where we invited teachers to discuss challenges and generate ideas for working together. The leadership team worked to restructure the professional development schedule, allowing more time for teacher collaboration during the school day. By respecting teachers' time and letting go of the expectation that they should use their planning periods for collaboration, teachers began to work more closely with colleagues from different grade levels. This led to increased collaboration and idea sharing, and resulted in greater alignment and consistency for students.

Step 6: React.

Teacher support can encompass proactive and reactive measures. While proactive support involves creating a conducive environment and setting realistic expectations, reactive support involves acknowledging teachers' hard work and achievements and addressing their mental and emotional well-being.

Acknowledging teachers' efforts and successes can be as simple as offering verbal praise, writing notes of appreciation, or publicly recognizing their contributions. Such gestures boost morale and validate their dedication and hard work, fostering a positive work environment. Image 11.2 shows an example of a fun surprise for your staff to find in their mailboxes.

Image 11.2

Mental and emotional support is as important as recognition. This support can include mentorship programs, counseling services, and access to resources for self-care and well-being. Teachers face numerous challenges and experience stress and burnout. Offering mentorship opportunities where experienced educators provide guidance and support assists teachers in navigating these difficulties. Access to counseling services provides a safe space for teachers to express their concerns, seek advice, and manage their emotional well-being.

Principals and educational leaders should be prepared to equip teachers with the necessary tools and resources to cultivate mindfulness and a sense of well-being. This may involve providing access to mindfulness training, wellness programs, stress management techniques, and resources for maintaining a healthy work-life balance. By prioritizing teachers' mental and emotional well-being, we create a more sustainable and supportive educational environment.

OVERCOMING PUSHBACK

When teachers are called heroes, it suggests they are expected to handle anything; instead, we need realistic expectations. People may push back because they have positive intentions, but we can let them know about the negative impacts and invite conversation and mutual understanding.

There's nothing wrong with being a hero. The use of superhero symbolism is well-intended, conveying the idea that teachers use their powers to help and protect others. However, in isolation, it can reinforce the concept of teachers as lone saviors, negating the collaboration and hard work that go into education. Teachers are certainly here to help and protect others, but they cannot do it alone. Teachers rely on the support of all stakeholders to be successful and happy both within and outside of the classroom.

The superhero narrative is flattering. Superheroes are often portrayed as individuals who have dedicated their lives to a cause and work tirelessly to achieve their goals. Teachers also exhibit these qualities. While the superhero narrative does highlight the dedication and hard work required to be a successful educator, we must be careful as this narrative can also be limited and even detrimental; teachers are already under so much pressure. Instead, teachers want and need realistic targets for a better chance at work-life balance. Acknowledge the work behind the flash.

Everyone is just so sensitive. It's true. We are living in a time when everything feels polarizing. But this is not a dichotomy. Teachers are amazing, *and* they work hard. We can, however, emphasize the range of roles and perspectives within the teaching world. This helps humanize teachers and reiterate that education is a group effort and not isolated to the individual.

THE HACK IN ACTION

by Nikki Goldfelder, school counselor

Education is a field in which humans are at the center of the work, yet so often, we forget the humanity of educators. We set high expectations for educators, with attendance being one of them. We know that children are best served when their educators are present; however, that sometimes comes at the expense of the educator's mental and physical health. Educators can better serve the children in their care when they care for themselves first.

Personally, I have had two of the most challenging years of my life. I walked through my mother's battle with cancer that she ultimately lost, and the emotional weight of that journey resulted in my own significant health challenges. While I knew I needed to be with my family and take care of my health, I experienced guilt about not being able to be present for my students and colleagues.

Dr. Erika Niles reassured me that the school team would rally around me and make sure my students had the support they needed in my absence. The stance she took allowed me to focus on what I needed to in a time of crisis.

However, it was not only because she supported me that I was able to balance my personal and professional needs. Dr. Niles fostered a strong school community through intentional interactions and relationship-building that made it possible for me to take the time I needed to be present for my mom and allow my mind and body to heal in the months that followed. Instead of expressing frustration that I missed a lesson, other teachers asked me how they could deliver social-emotional learning and also checked in on my family and me.

In a community that prioritizes belonging, there are times when each of us needs support and times when we give support to others. The pieces of us that make us human also pull us away from our work sometimes, and Dr. Niles supports that, knowing that by taking care of ourselves and our families, we can be more present and effective at school when we are there.

Because I was able to take the time I needed, I came back with the capacity to be much more effective for my students.

Administrators can view teachers as humans instead of heroes to create a supportive and collaborative school culture that recognizes the individuals and their unique circumstances. The world is ever-changing, and humans are unique. Realistic targets and expectations motivate teachers, provide direction, and help them achieve a sense of accomplishment.

Realistic targets also enable teachers to focus on specific areas for improvement and encourage ongoing professional development, which helps to eliminate the idea that we have to do it all—right now. By recognizing teachers' humanity and setting achievable targets, you foster a culture of innovation, creativity, and teamwork, resulting in better outcomes for teachers and students.

Treating teachers as everyday people is not about lowering expectations but changing them to focus on what is relevant and achievable. It's also about developing teachers as people, not making them into superheroes. We have to make it okay for teachers to be tired and fail and to not always be enthusiastic. With that, however, comes the responsibility of principals to make circumstances better without relying on the people experiencing these challenges to fix it all.

CONCLUSION
Become the Leader Your Teachers Need

W E NEED TEACHERS. After all, teaching is the profession that makes all other professions possible. That's not just a tagline or a bumper sticker; it's something I truly believe. Still, we are losing teachers at alarming rates. Universities are witnessing a decline in enrollment in all education-related programs. In my experience, colleagues and friends have dissuaded their kids from pursuing a teaching career. People contemplating education or beginning a career in education soon realize they can find a different kind of job with fewer demands, less stress, and more support and resources.

If we want to retain our educators, we need to help change the belief system. Throughout this book, I use the word "we" because I know that I, too, need to let go of what I thought the role of a principal should be in order to become the leader my staff needs. As somebody with a background in curriculum and instruction, this is hard, but whether we like it or not, the pandemic shifted what teachers want from principals. Teachers want realistic targets so they can strike a better work-life balance, they want distractions minimized, and they want social-emotional support. While that may feel like a lot, it is nothing compared to what teachers provide to our society.

Many times, principals ask teachers to remember their *why*. I am guilty of doing this. But teachers already know their why: it's kids and their learning. The problem is that teachers can't access their why because of so many barriers. It's up to us as building leaders to remove the barriers so teachers can help their students in a place where everyone feels psychologically safe.

To do that, we need to remember what it was like to be a teacher. For some of us, it's been a while. If we can't remember, we need to ask our teachers what they need to help them access their why. And, most importantly, we need to listen ... without the intent to reply and without judgment. To do this, we need to create the conditions where teachers feel safe being open and honest.

Remember that your teachers want to be seen as humans whose basic needs are considered. Though often told with good intentions, the narrative that teachers are superheroes or magicians can be harmful. Teachers are hardworking humans who need the help and support of their administrators to minimize distractions, set realistic targets, and help prioritize work-life balance. Teachers want to be cared for, thought of, seen, and appreciated.

People-centered leadership is hard ... and it matters. We must put our teachers first, which might mean our idea of a building leader is different than what we thought it would be, and our roles become more about what our teachers need rather than what we want. Being a great principal means prioritizing people over paperwork. It means being intentional about building trust and psychological safety. It means being consistent and having our actions match our words.

Strong administrator-teacher relationships thrive on trust. To *have* an authentic connection, we need to *be* authentic. If you don't love people and believe their potential is limitless, this book will do you no good. It's our job to love and believe in kids, and we can show that by supporting the adults whose daily work helps our kids succeed.

Being a leader is a tough job. It's easy to get caught up in the day-to-day obstacles. However, people-centered leaders don't let that happen. Instead, we aim to see obstacles as opportunities. We try to find what's right and fix what's wrong. It's about taking the fall and giving the credit.

In addition to serving our staff, we can invest in their growth by providing feedback, which may look different from traditional professional learning. Rather than focusing on all, we must focus on each. To do so, we need to know who our teachers are, the different ways in which they identify, how they want to be appreciated, and what they need to feel successful. Administrators need to commit to these learnings.

Being people-centered does not mean students aren't the focus. They are. We all got into this profession to support students. Our move out of the classroom allows us to focus on supporting the adults so they can support the kids. While our sphere of influence as principals might not be as deep regarding students, it is wide. And we can use that influence to help teachers feel safe to be their authentic selves so they can best serve our students. While we can't get rid of all the distractions, initiatives, and barriers, we can fit them into the work we are already doing, allaying stresses, encouraging growth, and keeping our teachers' focus on their most important priorities.

One of the most significant caveats of this book is that each school's staff is different. Each district is different. We can't have generic thinking when it comes to people-centered leadership. We must consider who is in front of us and what they need.

And therein lies the true Hack of *Hacking School Leadership* ...

know your people deeply. Take every opportunity to learn about the people you are lucky enough to serve, and you will serve them well.

While I have spent most of my words giving suggestions about what to do, I want to finish this book by amplifying another voice that shares the impact of a leader who provided what this teacher needed.

ONE LAST HACK IN ACTION

by Michael Bissel, educator

Two things resonated with me in working with Mrs. B. She believed that culture was built through trusting relationships, and she believed strongly in autonomy. In essence, "Hire good people, and get out of their way!"

She exemplified the servant leader. I had no idea the impact she would have on my career, but it began with a simple introduction. I was hired to be a classroom teacher at a new magnet school. In those frenetic weeks before school started in the fall, my eldest daughter walked with me into the building, where I introduced Mrs. B as my boss. Mrs. B smiled, took my daughter's hand, and said explicitly, "I work with your father." It was in that moment that I realized I had found my place in education where I could grow and develop as a servant leader through her example.

In the coming years, I would transition out of the classroom and into the role of instructional leader and curriculum coordinator. I took each step with the support and trust Mrs. B had in me. She supported my development for several years before she announced her retirement. She pulled me aside after her announcement and told me I had a servant's heart and should go into educational leadership.

The experience I had in her presence changed my trajectory in teaching and learning. She built a culture of trust through her service to others. Her motto was "Happy teachers make happy students!" And she was right. The happiness I experienced helped to create happiness and success in our students, and together, we worked to build the top elementary school in the state.

All because she was the leader I needed.

ABOUT THE AUTHOR

DR. ERIKA GARCIA-NILES has served as an elementary and middle school teacher, literacy coach, math specialist, instructional coordinator, and elementary principal. She is the principal at the best school in the world, Green Trails Elementary of the Parkway School District in Chesterfield, Missouri. Erika holds a BA in Elementary Education from Maryville University, an MS in Elementary Education from Lindenwood University, an MS in Education Leadership from Southwest Baptist University, and an EdD in Educational Leadership from the University of Missouri-St. Louis.

Erika is active on X (@flyingmonkey13) and also serves as a chauffeur for her three brilliant soccer-playing children.

ACKNOWLEDGMENTS

AS A PERSON who appreciates words, I take the responsibility of using them to express gratitude very seriously. This book would not have been possible without Mark Barnes, Jennifer Marshall, Regina Bell, Jennifer Jas, Steven Plummer, and the entire Times 10 Publications team. From identifying me as someone with the potential to share my ideas to helping me through this process while writing a dissertation, they trusted me, and I am so grateful.

To my beautiful and wonderful family, Darren, Henry, Eddie, and Maria. Thank you for your patience as I sat home with a keyboard in my lap, listening to *The Golden Girls* as I vacillated between work, grad school, and writing. Your unconditional support and encouragement are felt, loved, and cherished.

To my dad, Lenny, and my mom, Linda, as well as my siblings, Jennifer and Daniel. Thank you for your love and belief in me. Most importantly, thank you for keeping me laughing.

My amazing father-in-law, Rich, and my late mother-in-law, Jan, certainly deserve a shout-out for raising a wonderful father who has run our household so I could pursue my dreams.

My loudest cheerleader, Kathleen Mercury. My brilliant co-researcher, Kristen Pelster. Thank you both for being two of the strongest, most brilliant women I know.

To my staff at GT. You have inspired me not only in the work that shaped this book but in my life. I am better because of each of you. Thank you for loving me and for loving one another.

Finally, to educators ... thank you. Thank you for being a part of the profession that makes all other professions possible. To those who were strong enough to stay and to those who were strong enough to walk away, thank you. This job is hard, and we need leaders who will continue to remove the barriers so we can meet the needs of every student.

SNEAK PEEK

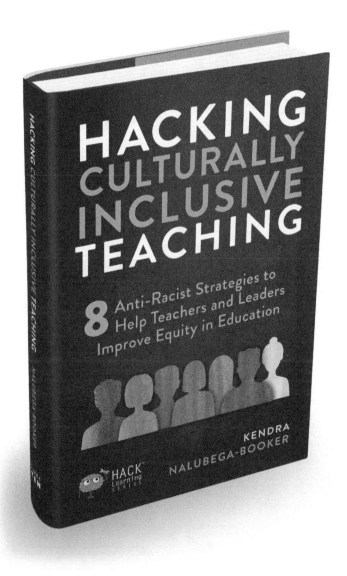

HACK 1

SHIFT TOWARD BRAVE SPACES

Design an Authentic Environment

THE PROBLEM: CLASSROOMS ARE NOT ALWAYS SAFE SPACES FOR RACIALIZED STUDENTS

O FTEN, WHEN RACIALIZED students express strong emotions and views or share harsh glimpses of their everyday experiences, members of the dominant group may feel unsafe, become uncomfortable, or react defensively. This further pushes students and teachers into comfort zones that get in the way of real learning or confronting issues that go beyond classroom boundaries. Even if your school doesn't allow you to directly address the issues, the way you treat students will impact how they perceive each other outside of the classroom.

The difference between a safe space and a brave space is that a safe space is historically created and guarded by racialized communities—and they protect it by dictating who can and cannot be in these spaces. On the other hand, brave spaces can be any space that challenges anyone to participate honestly in sensitive topics, even with the risk of becoming problematic or offensive. The phrase "safe space" became loosely used and sometimes confused with "brave space." In a safe classroom, students and teachers can participate in thought-provoking conversations without being held accountable when they offend others or perpetuate racism or other-isms because it is "safe"—unlike brave spaces, which allow for accountability and responsibility for what we say and do.

Although it is easier to maintain the traditional curriculum, we miss out on truly supporting our students, whose histories and current realities misalign with the "traditional" curriculum. True transformation comes from pushing limits and challenging ourselves and our students to grow. We need more "brave" classroom spaces, making it a top priority for us to create these spaces and set a firm foundation for inclusive teaching.

THE HACK: SHIFT TOWARD BRAVE SPACES

First used by Brian Arao and Kristi Clemens in their book *The Art of Effective Facilitation: Reflections from Social Justice Educators*, the term "brave spaces" has since gained widespread usage. They suggested five key components to creating a brave space in education.

- Controversy with civility encourages students to express their opinions while respecting others' perspectives, despite their differences.

- When owning intentions and impacts, students consider how their words have affected the emotions of others.

- Students engage in conversations that may be challenging for them when they opt to be challenged by choice.

- Students practice respect or mutual regard for one another's dignity as human beings.

- Students agree to not maliciously inflict harm on one another when they commit to the no attacks component.

When teachers and students allow themselves to be vulnerable in class, they actively choose to foster more meaningful connections between themselves and their peers. To meet the challenges as educators, we can work to unlearn problematic perspectives and ideas that lead to unjust actions.

You can transform your classroom into a brave space. Position it by setting classroom rules or codes: what you allow and what you don't. Promote critical thinking, growth, and empathy.

As educators, we can recognize that all students bring unique experiences and backgrounds to the classroom and that they can all learn from each other. In the same sense, we realize that not all experiences are equal, especially when it comes to the lived experiences of racialized students. Let's aim for holistic education: asking about students' languages and cultures, engaging them, sparking conversations about current events, promoting diverse ways of learning, and challenging students to think critically on a local, national, and global level. While not all schools and districts allow teachers to delve into the more controversial issues, most teachers can subtly get the point across by allowing students to share their experiences with each other.

WHAT YOU CAN DO TOMORROW

- **Reflect on the answers to big-picture questions.** What would a brave space mean for my students? How should I prepare? How will such a space impact my teaching? What challenges should I expect? Do I have any ground rules for navigating difficult conversations? How do I handle sensitive topics in my classroom? Do my students feel comfortable participating? What needs to change? Who speaks up, and who is silent or silenced?

- **Set an example with an initial brave space activity.** Successfully turning your classroom into a brave space requires a long-term commitment, but you can begin tomorrow with this activity. Ask your students to sit in community-style circle seating, and start a conversation about what it means to be brave. You and your students can come up with a class definition based on responses. Ask students to think back to a time when they felt brave. Then, ask them to talk about the thoughts, images, feelings, or actions that came to mind. You could also ask them to create a project or image that shows a time when they were brave, even if it meant they might offend others. You may want to allow them to use their mobile devices, such as an iPad and an Apple Pencil, to create their images.

Ask students to explore the following questions:

▸ Have you ever done something brave at school? What was it, and why did you do it?

▸ For this classroom, what do you need to be brave?

▸ Go around answering the questions as a class and ask students to document responses in a shared Google document that everyone can access.

▸ Finally, ask the students to make a list of rules for being brave in the classroom based on what they have talked about and shared.

• **Explore goals for an open-minded environment.** It's essential to meet students where they are instead of setting unrealistic expectations. If you are new to transforming your classrooms in this way, use the SMART goal format to guide you (see Appendix A.1). That structure offers an extra piece of strategic planning that allows you to have tangible success measures as you implement this new approach. It is not always a necessary step for everyone, but it makes it easy for students to also set personal development goals. Ask yourself the following questions as you and your students set your goals:

▸ Does the objective identify a specific improvement area?

▸ Does it specify how to measure and evaluate success?

> ‣ Is it relevant to the creation and maintenance of a brave space?

> ‣ Is it constrained by a predetermined timeline?

- **Give and require mutual respect.** The classroom is a community that requires mutual respect, deep and critical thinking about human experiences, and a toolkit for students to use beyond the classroom. Students and teachers can use this toolkit to be allies to their racialized counterparts, and racialized students can exist without taking on a burden. By creating a brave space, we invite all conversations, difficult or not, and emphasize learning through honest reflections. This practice can be hard to navigate, but it is necessary because it allows students to connect societal experiences with learning and to develop skills beyond the classroom. It also amplifies the human experience that sometimes gets clouded when we shield students from the "real world" and avoid conversations about social injustices, educational inequities, and other forms of oppression that affect racialized students and teachers. While your school or district may not allow you to address any of these items directly, you can set up your students for success by discussing them outside of the school environment.

  Implement these idea starters with your students:

  > ‣ Listen to and value their thoughts and ideas.

  > ‣ Acknowledge and respond to their feelings.

▸ Treat all students equally and fairly.

▸ Use appropriate language and avoid sarcasm.

▸ Give students choices in learning activities and assignments.

▸ Encourage and praise their efforts and accomplishments.

▸ Respect their opinions and beliefs.

▸ Avoid making assumptions about their backgrounds.

▸ Involve students in problem-solving and decision-making.

▸ Respect their privacy and confidentiality.

- **Curate a list of questions to guide you as you create your first brave space classroom.** Brave spaces allow maximizing learning through others' experiences and recognizing counter-stories usually shared in safe spaces. Racialized students and teachers do not always feel comfortable sharing their stories, so put predetermined conditions in place for them to be vulnerable. We all can benefit from developing brave spaces; the next section provides ideas on how to integrate them into culturally inclusive and sustaining learning environments.

    Consider these examples:

    ▸ What are my expectations for student behavior?

    ▸ How can I create an environment that supports diverse backgrounds and opinions?

> ▸ What strategies can I use to foster a sense of trust and respect among my students?

> ▸ How can I encourage my students to feel comfortable speaking up and engaging in meaningful dialogue?

> ▸ How do I ensure accountability when students offend others?

> ▸ How can I promote collaboration and creativity in the brave space classroom?

> ▸ How can I make the brave space classroom an inclusive and safe space for all students?

> ▸ How can I create an atmosphere of acceptance and understanding?

> ▸ How can I address any issues of bias and discrimination that may arise?

> ▸ How do I use technology and other resources to enhance my brave space classroom?

- **Set up the classroom in a community-style circle.** Experiment with placements that bring everyone together. The community-style classroom format focuses on students working together to explore, discuss, and solve problems. This type of classroom approach encourages students to collaborate and learn from each other to reach a common goal. It also emphasizes communication, critical thinking, and problem-solving skills. In this format, students sit in a circle or around a table, allowing everyone an equal opportunity to participate. The teacher acts as a facilitator, helping students understand the concepts and come up with solutions. This type of classroom setting gives students the opportunity to learn from their peers and build relationships and trust. It is vital for students to belong to a community that is trusting, empathetic, and connected. Students should have the freedom to stand, lean, bounce, and move as they see fit.

Adjust furniture to create an inviting space that gives students more opportunities to interact with each other and actively participate in the learning environment, especially since racialized students may feel uncomfortable engaging in White-dominated, traditional classroom settings. Students benefit from having a choice since it gives them the freedom to work wherever and however they see fit. When they feel isolated, they are less likely to participate.

Make the environment more inviting by arranging desks in a semi-circle or full circle, with the teacher sitting among students. Include comfortable chairs and a desk arrangement that encourages conversation, with some desks facing each other. You can display student-created colorful art and inspiring posters on the walls. Scatter plants and small sculptures around the room. Help students to feel comfortable engaging in meaningful conversations in a relaxed and inviting atmosphere.

- **Explain why it's essential to establish brave spaces.** Once students understand what you are trying to create, they may start thinking about how and what they can contribute to this space. Their curiosity will spark, and they may have questions about what this means for them. Assure them this approach will enrich everyone's learning.

Choose a method of accountability. Abide by the rules or codes and ensure that everyone, including you, has access to the agreed-upon rules. You can choose to record your rules on a smart board or shared document where you can allow everyone to brainstorm ideas.

- **Model characteristics of a brave space.** When you are vulnerable or show empathy toward your students, they're more likely to follow your lead. This doesn't mean everyone must share opinions that they do not feel comfortable sharing. Instead, it invites students to share their ideas, feelings, and thoughts. They must challenge themselves to share as a way to enrich their learning. It also promotes honesty, trust, and a sense of community. More specifically, if someone says or does something deemed offensive, racist, or discriminatory, it should not be sugar-coated or brushed over to play it safe. Instead, address it and see it as an opportunity.

BUY
HACKING CULTURALLY INCLUSIVE TEACHING

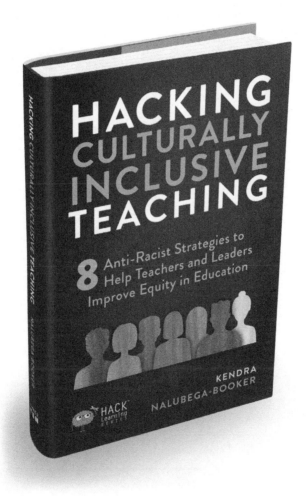

AVAILABLE AT:
Amazon.com
10Publications.com
and bookstores near you

MORE FROM
TIMES 10
PUBLICATIONS

Browse all titles at 10Publications.com

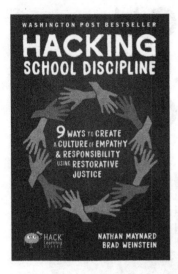

Hacking School Discipline

9 Ways to Create a Culture of Empathy & Responsibility Using Restorative Justice
By Nathan Maynard and Brad Weinstein

Reviewers proclaim this *Washington Post* Bestseller to be "maybe the most important book a teacher can read, a must for all educators, fabulous, a game changer!" Teachers and presenters Nathan Maynard and Brad Weinstein demonstrate how to eliminate punishment and build a culture of responsible students and independent learners in a book that will become your new blueprint for school discipline. Twenty-one straight months at #1 on Amazon, *Hacking School Discipline* is disrupting education like nothing we've seen in decades—maybe centuries.

Hacking Deficit Thinking

8 Reframes That Will Change the Way You Think about Strength-Based Practices and Equity in Schools
By Byron McClure and Kelsie Reed

Transform learning by reframing your view from what's wrong to what's strong. "At risk." "Low." "Title I kids." If you've worked with students, you've probably heard or said these coded labels that reflect deficit thinking. This focus on weakness is a pervasive, powerful judgment that continues to harm students long after they leave school. It's time for educators to hack deficit thinking. Unlearn student blame and reframe thinking to focus on student strengths, which will help everyone reach their highest potential.

Browse all titles at 10Publications.com

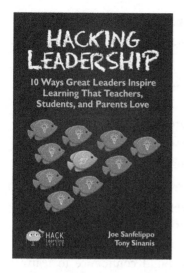

Hacking Leadership

10 Ways Great Leaders Inspire Learning That Teachers, Students, and Parents Love

By Joe Sanfelippo and Tony Sinanis

In this runaway bestseller, renowned school leaders Sanfelippo and Sinanis bring readers inside schools that few stakeholders have ever seen—places where students not only come first but have a unique voice in teaching and learning. The authors ignore the bureaucracy that stifles many leaders, focusing instead on building a culture of engagement, transparency, and most important, fun. *Hacking Leadership* has superintendents, principals, and teacher leaders around the world employing strategies they never before believed possible.

Hacking School Culture

Designing Compassionate Classrooms

By Angela Stockman and Ellen Feig Gray

Bullying prevention and character-building programs are deepening our awareness of how today's kids struggle and how we might help, but many agree: They aren't enough to create school cultures where students and staff flourish. This inspired Stockman and Gray to begin seeking out systems and educators who were getting things right.

"This book is chock-full of easy-to-implement actions that are kind to you, your students, and the environment you're creating in your classroom."

— Megan McDonough, CEO and Co-Founder, Wholebeing Institute

Browse all titles at 10Publications.com

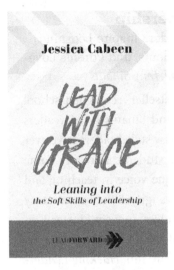

Lead With Grace

Leaning Into the Soft Skills of Leadership
By Jessica Cabeen

With technology, we interact with families, students, and staff 24/7, not just during the school day. Pressures can sway who we are into one who values online likes more than the authentic interactions that establish deep relationships with those we serve. School leader and keynote speaker Jessica Cabeen offers stories and strategies, practices and exercises, to empower teachers, principals, parents, and superintendents to build confidence to lean into the soft skills of leadership and lead with grace.

Hacking Life After 50

10 Ways to Beat Father Time and Live a Long, Healthy, Joy-Filled Life
By James Alan Sturtevant and Mark Barnes

Father Time is running scared, because life after 50 just got hacked! After-50s life used to be overwhelming. It made people think their best years were gone, even when they felt great and had a lot more to give. *Hacking Life After 50* shares 10 strategies you can use today to live a long, happy, joy-filled life and keep Father Time on the run. Sturtevant and Barnes show you how to create purpose in life's Act II; build momentum regardless of age; master meal planning; reclaim muscle, prevent injuries, and prolong functional movement; discover simple acts that promote healthy, happy living; sleep better than ever; and thrive now, tomorrow, and forever.

Browse all titles at 10Publications.com

RESOURCES FROM
TIMES 10 PUBLICATIONS
AND HACK LEARNING

10Publications.com

Connect with us on social media:
@10Publications
@HackMyLearning
Times 10 Publications on Facebook
Times 10 Publications on LinkedIn

TIMES 10 PUBLICATIONS provides practical solutions that busy people can read today and use tomorrow. We bring you content from experienced researchers and practitioners, and we share it through books, podcasts, webinars, articles, events, and ongoing conversations on social media. Our books and materials help turn practice into action. Stay in touch with us at 10Publications.com and follow our updates @10Publications and #Times10News.

51357835R00118